Sunset
Home Lighting
HANDBOOK

By the Editors of Sunset Books
and Sunset Magazine

Bright brass torchères, also shown on page 25.

Sunset Publishing Corporation
Menlo Park, California

Lighting up your home

Whether you're planning your overall lighting needs, looking for effective solutions to specific lighting problems, or seeking information on basic electrical circuitry, this book will meet your needs.

The first section offers guidance in determining what kinds of light you'll need, how much to use, and where to put it. In the middle section, we present an exciting array of colorful photographs showing lighting applications for every room in your home—and for outdoors, too. Finally, we show you how to wire it all together. You'll find step-by-step instructions for changing and installing fixtures and adding outlets and switches.

We wish to extend special thanks to Marianne Lipanovich for helping to research design and technical details and for scouting many of the photo situations; Jo-Ann Masaoka for location scouting and for styling a number of the photos; and Fran Feldman for her careful edit of the manuscript. Additional thanks go to Maureen Williams Zimmerman, Sarah S. Norton, and Michael Scofield for their editorial contributions.

Many others generously shared their lighting ideas, expertise, and examples. We'd particularly like to acknowledge Naomi Miller, Luminae, Inc.; Peggy Kass, IES; Kathleen Foote, Sylvania Lighting; and Joe Marcelli, Marcelli Lighting, Inc.

Cover: Outdoor and indoor lighting harmonize to create this striking scene. A movable underwater fixture spotlights the fountain; additional spots and built-in wall lights play on streams and pathways. Custom-designed fixtures on each outdoor column can be dimmed to suit the mood. Inside, banks of dimmable downlights brighten the living area; compact, movable uplights accent the indoor garden. Architect: The Steinberg Group. Landscape architect: Eldon Beck Associates. Photograph by Stephen Marley. Design by Roger Flanagan.

Book Editor
Scott Atkinson

Coordinating Editor
Suzanne Normand Mathison

Design
Roger Flanagan
Kathy Avanzino Barone

Illustrations
Bill Oetinger

Photographers
Russell Abraham: 22, 34. **Stephen Marley:** 1, 4, 18, 20, 21, 23, 25, 26, 27 left, 28, 29, 30 bottom, 31, 32, 33, 35 bottom, 36, 37 right, 38, 39, 40, 41, 44, 45, 47, 49, 50, 52, 53, 54, 55, 56 right, 57, 58, 59, 61, 62, 63, 64, 66, 67, 68, 70 right, 71, 75 top, 77 top, 79 top, 80. **Jack McDowell:** 37 left, 60. **Norman A. Plate:** 46. **Douglas Salin:** 43. **Michael Stokinger:** 2, 78 bottom. **Bill Ross:** 3, 27 right. **Tom Wyatt:** 24, 30 top, 35 top, 42, 48, 51, 56 left, 65, 69 top, 70 left, 72, 73, 74, 75 bottom, 76, 77 bottom, 78 top, 79 bottom. **Tom Yee:** 69 bottom.

Editor, Sunset Books: Elizabeth L. Hogan

Second printing December 1990

Hanging lanterns (see also page 78) were designed for candles. Now they're lighting up the garden.

CONTENTS

THE BASICS OF GOOD LIGHTING 4

Elements of Lighting Design •
Determining Your Lighting Needs • Light Bulbs & Tubes •
Selecting Light Fixtures • Lighting Up the Outdoors

ROOM-BY-ROOM LIGHTING INSPIRATION 18

Entries • Living Areas • Dining Areas • Kitchens •
Work Areas • Stairways • Hallways • Bedrooms •
Bathrooms • Outdoor Areas

WIRING IT ALL TOGETHER 80

Circuitry Considerations • Working with Wire •
Extending an Existing Circuit •
Installing Surface-mounted Fixtures •
Adding Recessed Downlights • Installing Track Systems •
Adding Plug-in Outlets • Wiring Switches & Dimmers •
Adding Outdoor Lights

Neon is for fun—here it accents a display
niche. For details, see page 27.

Pendants steal the show

Italian pendant fixtures and recessed downlights combine
to make this lighting scheme both eye-pleasing and functional. The hand-blown glass pendants are the focal point;
their silvered bowl bulbs cast a warm, ambient glow over
the breakfast table. The open downlights are unobtrusive
but hard-working: note how their placement follows the
lines of the center island and work counters exactly.
Interior design: Ruth Soforenko Associates.

THE BASICS OF GOOD LIGHTING

PLACEMENT • BULBS • FIXTURES

Good lighting design has an elusive quality; when you walk into an effectively lighted room, your eyes sense that everything is easily visible, but you'll rarely remark, "What fantastic lighting!"

That's because our eyes don't see the light itself, of course, but only see the objects on which it shines. Light serves as a silent partner in enhancing our surroundings.

Whether you feel that your home needs more light or you're planning lighting for a new house or addition, you'll find this book full of useful ideas. In this chapter you'll learn some of the elusive principles of good lighting design, how to determine the amount of light you need, and what light fixtures are available.

Once you have some ideas in mind, you may want to contact a lighting consultant, either for advice or for a complete plan, depending on your project and your budget. In many larger cities there are firms that specialize in lighting design (look in the Yellow Pages under "Lighting Consultants" or "Lighting Systems & Equipment"). Architects and interior designers may also list lighting as a specialty.

All three of these types of consultants usually belong to the Illuminating Engineering Society (IES).

Stores and electrical supply houses dealing in light fixtures may have in-house consultants, too.

When looking for help, keep in mind what kind of expertise you can expect from each type of professional. Lighting designers will calculate the light levels and beams needed in a given space, and then determine the fixtures and placement required. Architects often choose to highlight the special architectural features of a building while providing light for functional purposes. Interior designers, concentrating on total decor, will often choose fixtures for their decorative as well as functional value. If you're aware of these professional tendencies, as well as your own preferences, you can choose the type of professional with whom you'll work best. In any case, let your own style and needs be your guide.

ELEMENTS OF LIGHTING DESIGN

An essential ingredient in lighting design is simple common sense.

The best lighting designer is a problem-solver, determining where light is wanted and needed, and then putting it there with economy and flair. You can take the same approach using the following guidelines.

Three types of lighting

Today's designers separate lighting into three categories: task, accent, and ambient. Here's a quick definition of each type. (For an illustration of all three, see page 6.)

Task lighting illuminates a particular area where a visual activity—such as reading, sewing, or preparing food—takes place. It's often achieved with individual fixtures that direct light onto a work surface.

Accent lighting is similar to task lighting in that it consists largely of directional light. Primarily decorative, accent lighting is used to focus attention on artwork, to highlight architectural features, to set a mood, or to provide drama.

Ambient, or general, lighting fills in the undefined areas of a room with a soft level of light—say, enough to watch television by or to navigate safely through the room. Ambient lighting usually comes

5

Task lighting   Accent lighting   Ambient (general) lighting

from indirect fixtures that provide a diffuse spread of illumination. Directional fixtures can also be aimed at a wall to provide a wash of soft light.

Balancing & layering light

One rule of efficient lighting is to *put light where you want it*. But to ensure an attractive, comfortable lighting scheme, you also need to think about *balancing* light, that is, creating an effective spread of dim and strong light throughout the room.

The key to balancing is in layering light. Lighting designers first determine the focal point or points of the room (having two or three focal points is usually best). This is where they direct the brightest layer of light. Next, they add a middle layer to provide interest in specific areas without detracting from the focal points. The last layer fills in the background.

The first two layers are usually met with task or accent lighting, depending on what is being lit. The "fill" light is usually indirect. The ratio between the brightest light in the room and the fill light should be about 3 to 1, or at most 5 to 1. Ratios of 10 or even 100 to 1 are great for creating high drama, but they're too uncomfortable for everyday living.

Dimmers and control panels can help you custom-tailor light for multiple uses and decorative ef-

fects. Dimmers (also called rheostats) enable you to set a fixture or group of fixtures at any level from a soft glow to full-throttle. They're also energy savers. Control panels allow you to monitor up to nine or so functions from one spot. Originally designed for commercial use, they're now showing up in residential lighting schemes, too.

Beware of glare

One of the most important considerations in the placement of light fixtures is the glare they produce. Direct glare—a bare light bulb—is the worst kind. Deeply recessed fixtures or fixtures with black baffles or pinhole apertures (see page 15) will help remedy the problem. The interior surface finish of the reflector can also affect the amount of glare. Clip-on louvers and shutters, like those shown on page 14, help cut glare.

Watch for reflected glare, too—light bouncing off an object into your eyes. Light reflects off an object at the same angle it hits it. If the angle is too steep, the light produces a hot spot. The safety range is about 30° to 45°. (An example of a 30° angle is shown on page 9.)

If a fixture is located directly over a flat, shiny surface—for instance, a dining room table—veiling glare can be a problem. Objects on the table can deflect this glare; dimmers also help reduce the light level until it's comfortable.

Reflectance: The key to general light levels

How the color and texture of the walls, ceiling, and floor of a room contribute to the general light level depends on their reflectance—that is, the degree to which they reflect the light shed on them by windows and fixtures. The color and texture of the objects within a room also affect the overall light level.

Colors containing a lot of white reflect a larger amount of light, of course, and darker colors absorb light. A white object reflects 80 percent of the light that strikes it, while a black object reflects only 5 percent or less.

For this reason, if you were to redecorate your living room by covering creamy white walls with a rich blue wallpaper, you'd soon find that you needed more light sources and higher wattage bulbs to get the same light level as before. The illumination in a room with light-colored walls is distributed farther and more evenly as the light is reflected from surface to surface, until it gradually diminishes.

Texture plays a less important role in reflectance than color does. Matte finishes diffuse light; smooth, glossy finishes bounce light directly away, reflecting it onto other surfaces. Thus, a room with fabric-covered walls will require more or brighter light than a room with painted walls if it's to achieve the same level of light.

Color rendition

The color of an object as we perceive it is determined by two things: the surface color of the object and the color contained in the light shining on it. The color of a blue vase under a blue light will be heightened as the color of the light intensifies the color of the vase. Under a red light, the same blue vase will appear dull and grayish, because the red light waves are absorbed, and there are no blue waves to be reflected by the vase. This interaction between an object and a light source is called color rendition.

Light sources give off varying amounts of color. *Daylight*, or *sunlight*, appears white, but it actually contains the full spectrum of colors. *Incandescent light* includes colors from most of the spectrum but has a large proportion of yellow and red. When dimmed, incandescent light becomes even more red.

Fluorescent light is generally thought to be low in red and high in green and blue light waves, but, in fact, there are more than 200 "colors" of fluorescent tubes available. *Quartz halogen* produces brighter, "whiter" light than

either incandescent or fluorescent; it's popular for commercial display and museum lighting, as well as for residential use.

Light bulbs are formally rated by *color temperature*, measured in degrees Kelvin (K). Temperatures below 3,500°K are reddish or warm; higher temperatures are increasingly blue. The chart below, at left, shows the position of several standard light sources on the scale.

Because lighting can affect the apparent color of fabrics and wallpaper, it's always a good idea to choose furnishings and decorating materials under the same type of light you'll be using in your home. If possible, bring a swatch of material or a paint sample home. Or you can take it to a lighting store. Today's "light labs"—showrooms where you can directly compare light sources—make this process a lot easier.

How much light do you need?

Comfortable light levels are a matter of individual preference. Some people who work in brightly lighted offices grow accustomed to this kind of environment and want the same level of light in their homes. Other people feel more relaxed and secure in relatively low light levels, preferring to illuminate primarily the area in which they're reading, working, or relaxing.

For many years Americans have lived in relative brightness indoors—the light levels recommended by our lighting engineers have been much higher than those recommended in Europe. But with the new accent on energy conservation, our engineers are scaling down recommended levels. The trend now is toward providing bright lighting in task areas, with surroundings more softly lit, rather than trying to achieve uniform brightness.

Factors that affect light levels. When you're determining how much light is needed for a given activity, weigh these factors: 1) the difficulty of the task to be performed, 2) the speed and accuracy with which it must be completed, 3) the color contrasts among the materials involved in the task, and

4) the eyesight of the person who will be engaged in the activity.

If an older person will be doing embroidery on a dark cloth with richly colored thread, for example, lots of light will probably be required; the task calls for a high degree of accuracy, and the weak contrast between the fabric and thread is hard on older eyes. For less demanding visual activities, such as reading the newspaper or watching television, light levels can be much lower.

Measuring lumens. One method for measuring and planning light levels involves adding up the amount of light, measured in *lumens*, emitted by all the bulbs in a certain area. If you look at the sleeve around a light bulb, you'll see that it states both the bulb's wattage (the amount of electricity used by the bulb) and the number of lumens, or amount of light, that the bulb produces.

As a rule of thumb, the most difficult visual tasks, such as embroidery, require a total of at least 2,500 lumens in an average room, with the greatest number of lumens concentrated at the work location. A casual task, such as watching television, requires from 1,500 to 2,000 lumens. To find the number of lumens available in a given room, area, or lighting plan, add up the lumen outputs of all the bulbs in that area.

For close, precise work, you might want a table lamp with a three-way bulb switched to high, providing 2,250 lumens, immediately next to the work area, while another nearby lamp with a 60-watt bulb adds another 850 lumens. Roughly the same total of lumens could also be supplied by two 100-watt bulbs or four 60-watt bulbs, arrayed around the work area, but common sense calls for a greater concentration of light at the work area.

General light levels. Though providing enough light for task areas is of primary importance, remember to light the surrounding areas with accent and/or ambient light. If these areas were not at least softly lighted, whenever you looked up your eyes would have to compensate for the change between light levels, resulting in eyestrain.

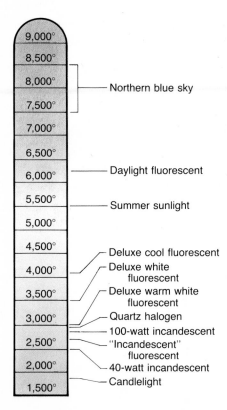

- 9,000°
- 8,500°
- 8,000° — Northern blue sky
- 7,500°
- 7,000°
- 6,500°
- 6,000° — Daylight fluorescent
- 5,500° — Summer sunlight
- 5,000°
- 4,500° — Deluxe cool fluorescent
- 4,000° — Deluxe white fluorescent
- 3,500° — Deluxe warm white fluorescent
- 3,000° — Quartz halogen
- — 100-watt incandescent
- 2,500° — "Incandescent" fluorescent
- 2,000° — 40-watt incandescent
- 1,500° — Candlelight

DETERMINING YOUR LIGHTING NEEDS

The first step toward improving your lighting involves careful consideration of the design and layout of your rooms and the types of activities that take place in each one.

If you're planning new lighting, you may want to draw a basic room plan (if you're building or remodeling, you can trace your architect's plans). Note the location of some basic furnishings on your plan, as well. These sketches will help you determine where to place your fixtures, what kinds to use, and where you'll want new outlets or wall switches.

Lighting for active living

In working on your lighting plan, you'll find that some areas—including hallways, stairs, entries, closets, laundry areas, and workshops—host only one type of activity. These areas are the simplest to plan for; often, one level of light and one set of fixtures will be sufficient.

Family rooms, living rooms, and other multiple-use areas, such as great rooms, will present more of a challenge. Today's family room may be the site of such diverse activities as television viewing, entertaining, piano playing, reading, and model making. The light levels required for these activities range from very soft ambient light to strong directional task lighting.

Just as all of these activities aren't likely to be going on at the same time, you probably won't wish to have all the room's specialized lights on at once. What will be needed is a variety of light levels, sources, and controls.

To begin, look at the areas in your multiple-use rooms where the more exacting visual tasks are undertaken. If your family enjoys model making or working on puzzles at a table that doubles as a snacking area when you're entertaining, you might want a pendant fixture with a strong light controlled by a dimmer; the high wattage can be used whenever puzzles or models are in progress and the dimmer used during entertaining.

An adjustable floor lamp or short track system above the piano can light both sheet music and the surrounding area when your piano student is at work. For reading or sewing, you can place a table or floor lamp with a three-way bulb next to an easy chair.

Lighting architectural features

You can use light both to complement the special architectural features in your house and to help disguise some aspects you'd like to downplay. As you walk through your house or go over your plans, try to focus on some of the ways light can work for you.

Ceilings can pose special problems or become special features. If your ceilings seem too low, bounced indirect light from uplights, torchères, or coves can help "raise" them.

"Raising" a ceiling with uplighting

Another common problem in older homes is rough or patchy ceiling plaster. For this problem and for ceilings that seem too high, the solution is the same: keep light off the ceiling surface by using downlighting, either from surface-mounted (not recessed) fixtures or pendant fixtures. The darker surface will seem lower, and imperfections will go unnoticed.

Masonry surfaces, such as brick walls or a stone fireplace, take on new beauty and importance when lighted at an angle to play up their textures.

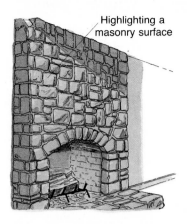

Highlighting a masonry surface

Room dimensions can "change" as a result of tricks played by light. Small rooms can become open and airy; large rooms can be made to appear cozy and inviting.

In a small room, washing the walls with an even layer of light seems to push them outward, expanding the space. If the wall is light colored, the effect is greater.

A large room illuminated with a few soft pools of light concentrated on important objects or areas becomes smaller and more intimate, as the lighted areas demand more attention than the room as a whole.

Narrow rooms benefit from trickery, too: lights along shorter walls draw the eye away from long ones, resulting in a "wider" space.

Cathedral or beamed ceilings can take on new importance with uplighting from coves or well-placed spotlights. Many designers are using beams to hold track lighting, taking advantage of architectural lines to disguise the lengths of track.

Mirrors should be lit from both sides to eliminate shadows. If there's no wall space for installing fixtures, try mounting wall sconces or strip lights directly on the glass. In a bathroom, you could substitute a continuous fluorescent strip along the top (be sure to choose one in a flattering color).

Windows, sources of daylight, can pose problems at night, when they seem like dark mirrors or black holes if left uncovered. Bright diffusing lamps or fixtures can produce annoying glare and reflection in the glass.

One way to avoid reflections is to light the area outside the window to a high enough level that lights inside balance with those on the outside. This use of outdoor lighting also gives the effect of extending your living area.

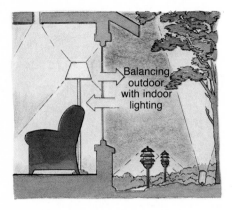
Balancing outdoor with indoor lighting

Another solution is to use opaque pendant fixtures or recessed downlights; then, only the lighted areas can be seen, not the light sources.

Window seats with small built-in downlights or wall fixtures can become cozy corners at night.

Skylights with fixtures concealed behind diffusing panels, like the one shown on page 45, can give a feeling of continuing daylight, instead of becoming dark holes at night.

Solar rooms with a large bank of windows on the south or west side require some artificial light during certain times of day to counteract the contrast between the brightness of the sunlight and the shadows the sun produces.

Alcoves or niches lighted with a warm glow turn into focal points at night, for display or for simple variation in design.

Decorative features to consider

As you think through your home's lighting scheme, you'll want to consider several aspects of each room's decor. Basic design features, such as color (see page 6), the placement of furniture, and the display of decorative art, can make a difference in the placement, quality, and quantity of light you'll need.

Furniture placement dictates certain lighting needs. Consider the use of each piece of furniture in a given area. You may want wall fixtures above your buffet for serving and for ambient light. A freestanding wardrobe can be illuminated by a downlight for easier clothing selection.

Indoor plants need light to help them look their best—*and* to help them grow. Some plant lovers mix one watt of incandescent for every three watts of fluorescent light; a more convenient solution is to purchase special "grow bulbs."

You can silhouette plants with concealed uplights or by backlighting them against a luminous panel or lighted wall. Light bounces down through the foliage when a fixture is recessed in the ceiling or suspended from it. Fluorescent fixtures or strip lights mounted vertically on a wall provide even light for vines or indoor trees.

Artwork can be lighted in a variety of ways. For the most dramatic effect, spotlight works of art individually from above or below: a 30° angle is best—even less if you wish to play up the texture of an oil painting or woven hanging.

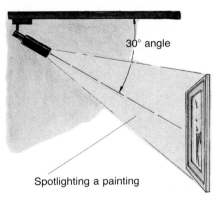
30° angle
Spotlighting a painting

Frame-mounted picture lights are another option, though these may not illuminate a painting evenly. A more economical way to light a group of pictures is by wall-washing evenly from above.

Sculpture and other three-dimensional objects usually call for lighting from both sides to minimize shadows. However, you can also emphasize shadows or a silhouette by aiming a single spot from behind or below. Don't hesitate to experiment to achieve the results you want.

Collections of books and records are best lit evenly; other items may require individual spotlighting. Fluorescent tubes or light panels produce the most even glow; cannisters and mini-tracks are best for accenting.

Downlighting may result in top shelves casting shadows on the shelves below. Backlighting, vertical lighting from the sides, or lights attached under the front edges of shelves will eliminate this problem. Concealed fixtures help keep glare out of people's eyes and lend a clean look to your display.

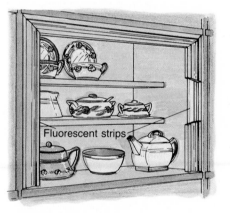
Fluorescent strips

Filling in dark areas

Once you've provided for adequate task and accent lighting, you should plan for some ambient, or general, light to soften the contrast between these light sources and the surrounding areas (see "General light levels," page 7).

Ambient light can be as simple as a diffused or dimmed fixture or lamp. It can also come from valances over curtained windows, fixtures bounced off the ceiling or walls, or indirect shelf or display niche lighting. Uplighting—in the form of cans, torchères, or built-in coves—creates an especially subtle touch in living areas.

LIGHT BULBS & TUBES

Light bulbs and tubes can be grouped in general categories according to the way they produce light.

Incandescent light, the kind used most frequently in our homes, is produced by a tungsten thread that burns slowly inside a glass bulb.

A-bulbs are the old standbys; these also come in three-way and long-life versions. *R*, *PAR*, and *ER* bulbs produce a more controlled beam; *silvered bowl* types diffuse light. A number of decorative bulbs are also available (see chart at right).

Low-voltage incandescent lighting for indoor use is new on the residential scene. Operating on 12 or 24 volts, these lights require transformers (which are often built into the fixtures) to step down the voltage from standard 120-volt household circuits. The small bulbs are especially useful in accent lighting, where light must be localized or precisely directed onto a small area. Low-voltage *mini-lights* are decorative in their own right.

Low-voltage fixtures are relatively expensive to buy; but in general, low-voltage lighting can be energy-efficient if carefully planned.

Fluorescent light is produced when electrical energy and mercury vapor create an arc that stimulates the phosphors coating the inside of the bulb. Because the light comes evenly from the entire surface of the tube, it spreads in all directions, creating a steady, shadowless light. Tubes require a ballast to ignite and maintain the electrical flow.

Fluorescent tubes are unrivaled for energy efficiency; they also last far longer than incandescent bulbs. In some energy-conscious areas, ambient lighting for new kitchens and bathrooms *must* be fluorescent.

Older fluorescent tubes have been criticized for noise, flicker, and poor color rendition. Electronic ballasts and better fixture shielding against glare have remedied the

		Type
Incandescent		A-bulb
	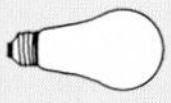	Three-way
	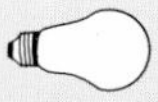	Long-life
		G—Globe
	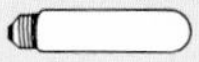	T—Tubular
		Flame-shaped
	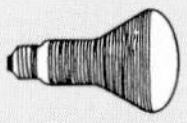	R—Reflector
		PAR—Parabolic aluminized reflector
	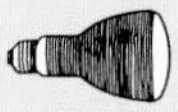	ER—Ellipsoidal reflector
		Silvered bowl
		Low-voltage reflector spot
	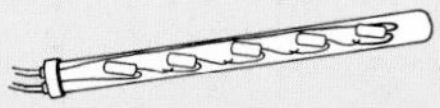	Low-voltage mini-lights
Fluorescent	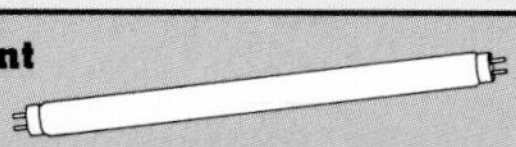	Tube
	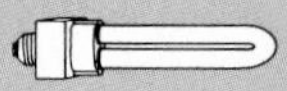	PL—Compact tube
	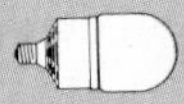	Compact
		Circle
Quartz halogen		High-intensity
	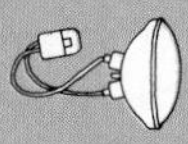	Low-voltage PAR
		Low-voltage MR-16 (mini-reflector)
High-intensity discharge (HID)		Mercury vapor
	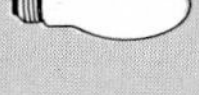	Metal halide
		High-pressure sodium

Description	Uses	Efficiency (lumens per watt)	Bulb life in hours	Watts
Familiar pear shape; frosted and clear.	Everyday household use.	12 to 21	750 to 1,000	4 to 300
A-bulb shape; frosted. Two filaments provide three light levels.	In lamps with special switches in multiuse areas.	11 to 15	1,000 to 1,600	30/70/100 to 100/200/300
A-bulb shape; frosted. Lasts longer but produces less light.	In hard-to-reach fixtures.	12 to 17	1,150 to 3,000	40 to 150
Ball-shaped bulb, 2″ to 6″ in diameter. Frosted or clear.	Often decorative; without shades or in pendant fixtures.	12 to 21	1,500 to 4,000	15 to 100
Tube-shaped, from 5″ long. Frosted or clear.	Appliances, cabinets, decorative fixtures.	7.5 to 10	1,000	15 to 60
Decorative; specially coated.	In chandeliers and sconces.	—	1,500 to 4,000	15 to 60
White or silvered coating directs light out end of funnel-shaped bulb.	In directional fixtures; focuses light where needed.	7 to 12.2	1,500 to 4,000	25 to 300
Similar to auto headlamp; special shape and coating project light and control beam.	In recessed downlights and track fixtures.	8 to 13	2,000 to 6,000	25 to 250
Shape and coating focus light 2″ ahead of bulb, then light spreads out.	Can replace higher-wattage bulbs in recessed downlights.	11.3 to 12.3	1,500 to 4,000	50 to 120
A-bulb in shape, with silvered cap to cut glare and produce indirect light.	Can be used in track fixtures and pendants.	—	1,000	60 to 200
Similar to standard R-bulb; directs light in various beam spreads and distances.	In low-voltage track fixtures and recessed downlights.	—	500 to 2,000	15, 25
Like Christmas tree lights; encased in flexible, waterproof plastic.	Decorative, to add sparkle.	—	22 years (est.)	0.84
Tube-shaped, 5″ to 96″ long. Needs special fixture and ballast.	Shadowless work light; also indirect lighting.	48 to 90	6,000 to 20,000	8 to 80
U-shaped with base; typically 5¼″ to 7½″ long.	Some PL tubes include ballasts to replace A-bulbs.	43 to 70	10,000	7 to 28
Resembles oversize A-bulb, has screw base; comes in variety of color temperatures.	Replaces A-bulb; uses far less energy. Fits any standard lamp socket.	43 to 60	5,000 to 9,000	13 to 21
6″ to 12″ circle. Some types require special fixtures; others can replace A-bulbs.	In compact circle fixtures.	48 to 70	12,000	20 to 40
Small, clear bulb with consistently high light output; used in halogen fixtures.	In specialized task lamps, torchères, and pendants.	18 to 22	2,000	100 to 500
Similar to auto headlight; tiny filament, shape, and coating give precise direction.	To project a small spot of light a long distance.	—	2,000	25, 50
Tiny (2″-diameter) projector bulb; gives small circle of light from a distance.	In low-voltage track fixtures and recessed downlights.	—	500 to 5,000	25, 50
Bulb-within-a-bulb, shaped like an oversize A-bulb; needs special ballast.	Available as garden and security lighting for residential use.	63	16,000 to 24,000	50 to 1,000
Similar to mercury vapor, almost twice as efficient; needs special ballast and fixture.	Outdoor security lighting. Now available in table lamp wattages with self-ballast.	115	10,000 to 20,000	175 to 1,500
Similar to mercury vapor. Gold-hued light. Needs special ballast and fixture.	Outdoor lighting; used indoors commercially and industrially.	140	10,000 to 24,000	35 to 1,000

first two problems; as for the last one, manufacturers have developed fluorescents in a wide spectrum of colors, from very warm (about 2,700°K) to very cool (about 6,300°K).

U-shaped *PL* fluorescents allow fluorescent light to be used in smaller, trimmer fixtures—for example, recessed downlights. *Compact* and *circle* fluorescents can replace A-bulbs: you simply screw the tube or a special adapter into a standard lamp socket.

Quartz halogen bulbs contain a tiny quartz filament that produces a brighter, whiter beam than other light sources. They're excellent for task lighting, pinpoint accenting, and other dramatic effects.

Halogen is usually low-voltage but may be standard line current. The popular *MR-16* bulb creates the tightest beam; for a longer reach and wider coverage, choose a *PAR* bulb. Both MR-16 and PAR bulbs are available in a variety of beam patterns, such as VNSP (very narrow spot), SP (spot), NFL (narrow flood), and FL (flood). An abundance of smaller bulb shapes and sizes serve other lighting needs.

Halogen's one disadvantage, besides the initial cost, is that it's very hot. Halogen bulbs require halogen fixtures. Be sure to shop carefully: some fixtures on the market are not UL-approved.

High-intensity discharge (HID) bulbs produce light when electricity excites specific gases in pressurized bulbs. Requiring special fixtures and ballasts, these lights may take up to 7 minutes to ignite after being switched on. The color emitted by some HID bulbs is rather unflattering, but they offer long life and high efficiency.

Neon light is also generated when electricity passes through a gas: neon gas, for example, glows orange red (other gases give off a variety of colors). Neon tubes' low light output makes them undesirable as a functional light source. Requiring a 24-volt transformer, neon fixtures can be expensive to buy, though they don't use much energy and may last for years.

Cold cathode, a close cousin of neon, puts out more light and is useful for general or indirect lighting as well as for decoration.

SELECTING LIGHT FIXTURES

Once you've determined the quality and quantity of light you need, you're ready to visit the local lighting, hardware, or electrical supply store—or are you?

Put off that trip for a bit and make it a point to observe the lighting around you in restaurants, stores, or a neighbor's house. Look for "living" examples of all the types of lighting presented in this book and sort out those you prefer from those you don't like. Then, with your needs and preferences in mind, you'll be ready to hunt for the fixtures that provide exactly the type of lighting you want.

Factors to weigh in choosing fixtures

If you've formed some ideas about the kinds of lighting you need, selecting fixtures would appear to be easy. But given the great variety available today, finding the right fixtures can be confusing and complicated. Here are some points to keep in mind.

Function. All types of lighting systems include fixtures that give strong directional light, general diffused light, or a combination. One of the primary considerations about any fixture is how it directs the light. Will it put the light you want where you want it?

Make sure that directional fixtures have a high enough maximum bulb wattage to allow you to use bulbs strong enough to "throw" the light from the fixtures to task or display areas.

Size. Fixtures on display will often look smaller in the store than they will in your home. Take measurements of your top choices; then find bowls or boxes of the appropriate sizes at home and hold them in place to determine if the fixtures you have in mind are the proper scale. Manufacturers often produce standard fixtures in graded sizes, so be sure to ask suppliers about other sizes.

Design. Here, personal taste will be your guide, leading you to

whatever suits your decor. Designers and architects have found that a sense of decorative continuity can be created by the use of similar fixtures throughout a home. In response to this, manufacturers offer "families" of fixtures available as spotlights, pendants, track lights, and ceiling fixtures.

Flexibility. Because tastes and habits often change, flexibility is an important consideration when choosing fixtures. If you change your display of artwork, you'll want to adjust your lighting, too.

Movable or adjustable lamps are longtime favorites partly because they're so flexible. With track systems, you can alter the location of fixtures along the track as well as the way each fixture is aimed. Even some built-in recessed downlights have changeable trim, so that a regular downlight can become a pinhole light or an eyeball.

Cost. You'll want to consider both purchase price and operating costs in selecting light fixtures. When a fixture is to be kept burning for several hours at a stretch, it may be wise to invest in a more costly low-energy unit than to buy a less expensive kilowatt-eater.

More expensive fixtures are likely to offer greater flexibility and higher engineering quality, producing more controlled light; you may want to use these in your living room or wherever such quality is important.

Maintenance. To operate efficiently, all fixtures should be cleaned regularly. Kitchens, bathrooms, and work areas demand fixtures that are easy to clean. Since all light bulbs must be changed eventually, consider using a simple fixture with a long-lived fluorescent bulb for the top of the stairs and other hard-to-reach spots.

Movable light fixtures

Table lamps, floor lamps, and small specialty lamps are easy to buy, easy to change, and easy to take along when you move. Within this category you'll find fixtures that will provide any quality of light you need.

Table lamps show individuality and style at the same time that

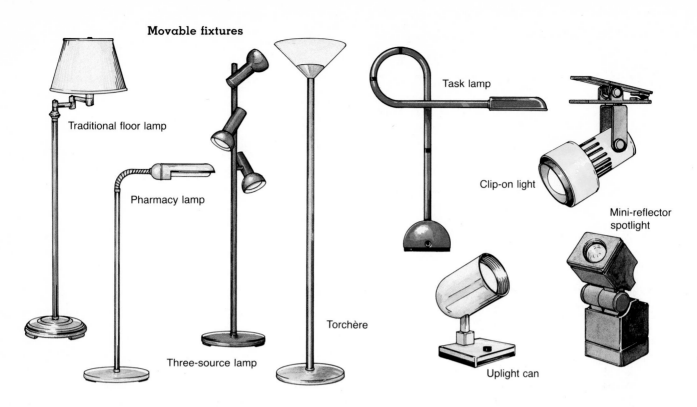

Movable fixtures

Traditional floor lamp

Pharmacy lamp

Three-source lamp

Torchère

Task lamp

Clip-on light

Mini-reflector spotlight

Uplight can

they serve as sources of light. Variety, mobility, and ease of installation add to the appeal of such lamps. Styles range from quietly traditional to brashly avant-garde.

The choice of a lampshade can be crucial to the effectiveness of a table lamp. A difference of only 2 inches in the diameter of the lower edge of the shade can make a significant difference in the spread of light shed by a lamp.

The height of the bulb within the shade also affects the circle of illumination: light will spread farther when the bulb is set low in the shade. Small extension screws used on the lamp harp to adjust the height of the shade are available at most lighting supply stores.

Floor lamps offer great flexibility. One type—the *traditional floor lamp*—often provides a combination of levels, serving either as a reading light or as a source of soft ambient light. Unobtrusive *pharmacy lamps* offer options, too, especially for tasks such as reading and sewing. Lamps with adjustable directional fixtures, such as *three-source lamps*, are a practical choice for task lighting.

Bright *torchères*, available in both halogen and incandescent versions, bounce light onto the

ceiling for a dramatic form of indirect lighting. However, the standard 8-foot ceiling is often too low for the typical 6- to 6½-foot-high torchère. In this case, look for a lamp with a built-in diffuser to avoid a hot spot. Some torchères include a dimmer unit for controlling the light output.

Specialty lamps in new varieties are constantly appearing on the market. These new lamps, like the traditional picture light and drafting table lamp, can fill a definite need while remaining movable, and they require no special wiring.

Easily adjusted *clip-on lights* are practical for providing task lighting over beds, desks, and shelves. *Uplight cans* highlight indoor plants or wash walls with light for instant decorating touches. *Mini-reflector spotlights* are handy for pinpointing paintings or sculpture from a nearby mantelpiece or shelf.

Adjustable task lamps supply a small, bright pool of light while leaving your immediate work area uncluttered. Halogen lamps produce the cleanest, tightest beam, while PL fluorescent models are tops for reducing glare and shadows.

Surface-mounted fixtures

Installed either on walls or on ceilings, surface-mounted fixtures (shown on page 14) are integral to most home lighting designs. Generally, surface-mounted fixtures can be added without a great deal of wiring work.

Ceiling and wall fixtures provide general illumination in traffic areas such as landings, entries, and hallways, where safety is a consideration. Kitchens, bathrooms, and workshops benefit from the added light from ceiling fixtures used in conjunction with task lighting on work surfaces.

Fixtures in this category range from functional frosted-glass globes to delicate, candlelike sconces. When selecting a fixture, look closely at the amount of light that bounces off the wall or ceiling to be sure the light will be directed where you want it. In some localities, new kitchens and bathrooms must be outfitted with fluorescent fixtures.

Wall sconces are great for hallways and for indirect lighting along walls. Place sconces about 5½ feet from the floor; keep them away from corners—otherwise, they'll create hot spots.

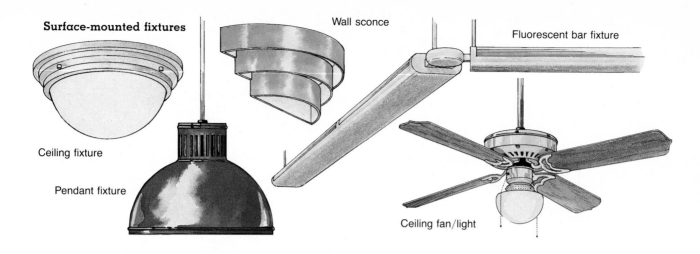

Surface-mounted fixtures

Ceiling fixture

Pendant fixture

Wall sconce

Fluorescent bar fixture

Ceiling fan/light

Chandeliers and pendant fixtures add sparkle and style in high-ceilinged entries and above dining and game tables. These decorative fixtures can give direct or diffused light—or a combination of the two—for different purposes.

The proportion of the fixture in relation to its surroundings is critical. If the fixture is used over a table, its width should be at least 12 inches less than the width of the table to prevent collisions with diners or passers-by. Hanging it about 30 inches above the table surface helps avoid glare. In an entry, be sure to allow enough room below the chandelier to guarantee safe passage for tall people.

Mini-lights and strip lights are partly for fun, partly for effective task lighting. They add a splash of light and color to display niches, kitchen counters, stair railings, bathroom mirrors, or just about anywhere else.

Track lighting

Track lighting offers great versatility and ease of installation. Available in varying lengths, tracks are really extended electrical lines from the outlets they plug into; fixtures can be mounted anywhere along each line.

A track can be flush-mounted or suspended, and used on ceilings or walls, often without the addition of extra wiring. Track fixtures should generally be close to the wall they're meant to light—within 2 to 4 feet. For safety, avoid track lighting in wet areas, such as bathrooms or laundry rooms.

Tracks come in one- and multi-circuit varieties; the multi-circuit type allows you to operate two or more sets of lights independently. Track connectors let you extend some systems indefinitely—in a straight line, at an angle, or even in a rectangle.

Tracks can accommodate pendant fixtures, clip-on lamps, and low-voltage spotlights, as well as a large selection of standard styles. Some low-voltage fixtures have an integral transformer; others fit a standard track with an adapter. Other tracks require an external transformer mounted away from the track (this transformer can serve several tracks and lights).

Accessories for track fixtures include filters, baffles, and louvers; all allow for greater light control. *Framing projectors* and *mini-tracks* (scaled-down systems for bookshelves) are especially effective for spotlighting artwork on a wall or shelf.

Recessed ceiling fixtures

Recessed downlights offer light without the intrusion of a visible fixture. For this reason, they're effective in rooms with low ceilings

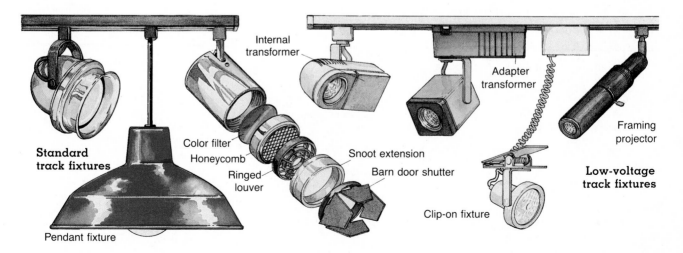

Standard track fixtures

Pendant fixture

Color filter

Honeycomb

Ringed louver

Internal transformer

Snoot extension

Barn door shutter

Adapter transformer

Clip-on fixture

Framing projector

Low-voltage track fixtures

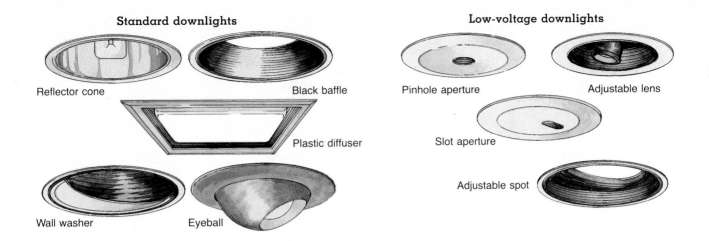

Standard downlights

Reflector cone

Black baffle

Plastic diffuser

Wall washer

Eyeball

Low-voltage downlights

Pinhole aperture

Adjustable lens

Slot aperture

Adjustable spot

and sleek lines. Basically a dome with a light bulb set in the top, a recessed downlight can be fitted with any one of a number of trims that aim the light to fit the function desired.

When used over sinks and countertops in kitchens, an *open downlight* spreads a strong task light over the work surfaces. Open fixtures are also good for lighting stairways and entries.

Equipped as a *wall-washer* fixture, a recessed downlight throws light onto a nearby wall; a series of such fixtures can be used for even, balanced lighting of a wall of artwork or bookcases. Normally, wall-washing fixtures are mounted in a series 3 feet away from the wall to be washed, with 3 feet between fixtures. To emphasize a wall's texture, position fixtures 12 to 18 inches from the wall and each other. (Or, for a scalloped effect, try a wider spacing.)

Adjustable *eyeball* or *elbow* fixtures highlight objects on a wall.

Low-voltage downlights — especially those with MR-16 bulbs and black baffles—are very popular for accent lighting. Like their track counterparts, many low-voltage downlights include an integral transformer; you can also use one external transformer to serve a number of fixtures.

Recessed fixtures can be added in existing ceilings, provided there's enough space between the ceiling and the floor or roof above. Fixtures range from 5¼ inches to more than 12 inches in depth, though some manufacturers offer shallower models for use in tight spaces.

Because glare can be a problem with downlighting, reflective interior finishes, baffles, lenses, and louvers have been developed to direct the light away from people's sight lines. In general, fixtures

with deeply inset bulbs will produce less glare.

Built-in indirect lighting

Coves, cornices, valances, wall brackets, and soffits can be used when indirect lighting is desired. Simple and architectural in design, these devices ensure that light sources are shielded from view, allowing light to spill out around the shields.

Coves direct light upward onto the ceiling, while *cornices* spread light below. Used over windows, *valances* send light both up to the ceiling and down over draperies. *Wall brackets*, mounted directly onto interior walls, spread light both up and down, and can be used to highlight artwork or to provide ambient light in living areas. *Soffits*, used over work areas, throw a stronger light directly below.

Built-in indirect lighting

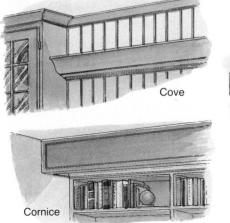

Cove

Cornice

Valance

Soffit

Wall bracket

LIGHTING UP THE OUTDOORS

Plan outdoor lighting, either 12 or 120 volts, much as you would indoor lighting. It's easiest to begin by deciding where you'll need light at night for safety, activity, and security. Then you can add decorative or festive lighting—though in many cases you can choose lights that will be both functional and decorative.

Eliminating glare

Regardless of the lighting you choose, you'll want to avoid glare from your fixtures. In effect, glare is the reason for the discomfort we feel when looking at a light that's too bright, or one that's aimed directly at us. At night, because the contrast between darkness and a source of light is so great, glare can be a persistent problem. Several methods of minimizing glare are discussed below.

Using shielded fixtures. In a shielded fixture, the bulb area is completely hidden by an opaque covering that directs the light away from a viewer's eyes. The eye sees the warm glow of a lighted object rather than a hot spot of light.

Placing fixtures out of sight lines. Another way to avoid glare is to place your fixtures either very low, as along a walk, or very high on a tree—and then direct them in such a way that only the light playing on the tree branches, and not a bright spot, is noticed.

Lowering light levels. Rather than using one high-wattage light at your front door, it's at once less glaring and more inviting to use several softer lights strategically placed in the front yard. A little light goes a long way at night: 20 watts is considered "strong," and even 12 watts can be very bright. If you're using line current, choose bulbs with a 50-watt maximum.

Low-voltage or standard current?

Because they're safer, more energy-efficient, and easier to install than standard 120-volt systems, low-voltage lights are often used outdoors. Such systems use a transformer to step down standard household current to 12 volts.

Installing a low-voltage system is simple: cable can lie on top of the ground, perhaps hidden by foliage; most fixtures connect easily to cables; and no grounding hook-ups are required. You won't need an electrical permit for installing a system that extends from a plug-in transformer (the most common kind).

In addition to the packaged low-voltage systems available, you can use low-voltage PAR spotlights to light trees or larger areas. Halogen MR-16s are increasingly popular for outdoor accent lighting.

But the standard 120-volt system still has some advantages outdoors. The buried cable and metallic fixtures give the installation a look of permanence. Also, light can be projected a great distance, especially useful for security and for lighting trees from ground level. An additional advantage is that power tools and patio heaters can be plugged into 120-volt outdoor outlets.

Lighting for safety & decoration

To evaluate your outdoor lighting needs, take a careful look at several areas around your property—along your driveway, front walk, and steps; around the front door and the back gate; on the deck or patio; around the swimming pool; and in planted areas.

Driveways, especially if they're long and wooded, should have some kind of lights to define their boundaries. Fixtures installed for this purpose should be low and soft enough to prevent glare in a driver's eyes. The garage area needs security lighting, preferably controlled by switches both inside and out. Downlights or carefully aimed spotlights cast a strong beam while reducing glare. Motion-sensitive lights mounted on a garage are also useful; the lights go out when no motion occurs within a preset time.

Front walks and steps are easiest to light if their surfaces are a light, reflective color. Low fixtures that spread soft pools of light can greet guests and highlight your garden's virtues along the walk.

Outdoor fixtures

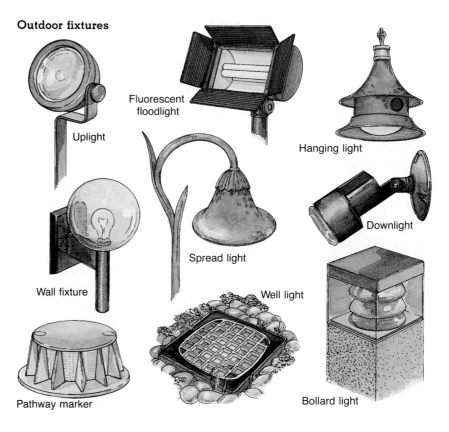

Uplight

Fluorescent floodlight

Hanging light

Wall fixture

Spread light

Downlight

Pathway marker

Well light

Bollard light

If your house has deep eaves or an overhang extending the length of your walk, you might consider installing weatherproof downlights to illuminate your walk and plantings without any visible fixtures.

Often, your steps will be adequately lighted by fixtures at the front door, but even single steps should be illuminated if they're any distance from the door. A small fixture above the steps will do, though you may be able to build in a light under the stairs or along a wall or railing.

At the front door, you'll want light for several purposes. In addition to lighting your house number and welcoming guests, you'll want light enough to see a caller's face. If you choose decorative clear glass fixtures, remember to keep low-wattage bulbs in them to avoid uncomfortable brightness.

Adequate lighting at the back gate and other house approaches gives a sense of security. You may wish to use spotlights mounted high on your house walls. As this kind of fixture directs a strong light, you can aim it to graze a wall, illuminating the area without glaring

directly in anyone's line of vision. Photocells are available that turn these lights on at dusk and off at dawn, to cut down on their high energy use as well as to provide security when you're away.

On decks and patios, a low level of light is often enough for quiet conversation or alfresco dining. By lighting steps, railings, or benches indirectly from underneath—or directly with strings of mini-lights—you can outline the edges of your structure for safety, too.

Don't forget to add stronger light wherever you do your serving or barbecuing. Downlights are a popular choice, but indirect lighting—diffused through plastic or another translucent material—is also useful.

Swimming pools and spas require special consideration, too. These areas should be lighted for safety and to make them attractive from inside the house.

Most pools have an underwater light in the deep end. To avoid glare, consider putting this on a dimmer, especially if the light is in view of the house or patio sitting area. For relaxing and enter-

taining, all the light that's needed is a soft glow to outline the pool edges, but the light should be on full brightness when children are swimming. Low spotlights muffled by foliage or trained on walls can provide dramatic indirect lighting, reflecting on the pool surface when the pool light is off.

Popular for an evening soak, a spa or hot tub can be illuminated with low-voltage twinkling mini-lights that will subtly outline its perimeter or steps.

Illuminating foliage can be an effective way to combine functional and decorative lighting. Uplighting, downlighting, and spread lighting are all common techniques.

For a dappled, "moonlight" effect, place both uplights and downlights in a large tree. To silhouette a tree or shrub, aim a spotlight or wall washer at a fence or wall from close behind the plant. Decorative mini-lights help outline trees and lend sparkle to your garden.

You can create a number of interesting garden effects by placing uplights, downlights, and accent lights on separate switches. Dimmers can be used for even more flexibility.

Outdoor lighting techniques

Downlighting

Moonlighting

Spread lighting

Path lighting

Diffused lighting

Silhouetting

Accenting

Accent on architectural lighting

Sparkling low-voltage mini-lights focus attention on the
striking high windows in this easy but elegant living
room. A concealed fluorescent fixture highlights the niche
above the mantel; the candles add a warm, festive tone.
Sleek brass lamps behind each sofa provide reading
light where and when it's needed. Floodlights on the
plantings outside seem to extend the boundaries of the
room, while their brightness eliminates reflections on
the glass inside. Architects: MLTW Turnbull Associates.
Lighting design: Richard Peters.

ROOM-BY-ROOM LIGHTING INSPIRATION

TASK • ACCENT • AMBIENT

This section of the book, a colorful gallery of lighting ideas, is designed to get your creativity flowing. It includes "enlightening" examples for every room of the house, from the entry to the basement workshop, covering a variety of design situations and lighting techniques. Also illustrated are designs for outdoor lighting.

Take a careful look

Though light is elusive and its effects are difficult to capture in photographs, spend a few minutes here with the photos that interest you. Look closely, and you'll discover a great deal.

Most of the photos were taken at night, with a minimum of photographer's lights, in an effort to let the lighting in each picture stand on its own. This should make it easier for you to judge what kind of light is actually present and exactly how it affects the environment. In some cases, the fixtures will be evident; in others, you'll see only the lighted surfaces. Try to look beyond the decor in each photo and consider the light itself, to see if it's playing tricks or if it's straightforward and simple.

Artist's sketches of some of the installations featured—where details weren't immediately evident in the photographs—have been included,

in case you'd like to adapt the same type of lighting to fit your needs. A number of these drawings include measurements, primarily to provide a sense of scale— your applications will probably call for different specifications. The wiring know-how necessary for installing most of the examples shown can be found in the wiring section at the end of the book.

Putting ideas into action

Whether you're building or remodeling, or you just want to see your house in a new light, you'll find guidance in the following pages. The section takes you on a room-by-room tour of the house and suggests ideas for lighting up the outside. The stops along the way include the following:

- Entries (pages 20–21)
- Living areas (pages 22–31)
- Dining areas (pages 32–39)
- Kitchens (pages 40–47)
- Work areas (pages 48–53)
- Stairways (pages 54–55)
- Hallways (pages 56–57)
- Bedrooms (pages 58–63)
- Bathrooms (pages 64–71)
- Outdoor areas (pages 72–79)

Each section begins with a "short course" on principles and strategies for dealing with that par-

ticular area. If you run across unfamiliar terms, you should be able to find an explanation in the first chapter. For special architectural problems—such as lighting a ceiling, stone fireplace, or bank of mirrors—turn to "Lighting architectural features" on page 8. "Decorative features to consider," page 9, suggests tips on accenting artwork, bookshelves, or indoor plants.

"Light labs"—where you can directly compare the effects of different light sources and fixtures— are very helpful for fixture shopping; so are well-stocked lighting showrooms. Of course, a lighting designer, architect, or interior decorator (see page 5) can greatly aid your efforts.

If necessary, you can also experiment at home with an inexpensive lighting kit you assemble yourself. A standard utility clamp lamp with a conical aluminum reflector (available at hardware stores) will approximate a pendant fixture or task lamp. A 1- or 2-pound coffee can with a socket inserted through the bottom mimics a downlight. Either borrow a table lamp from another room or cut a translucent shade for the clamp lamp from heavy white paper. You'll also need some standard household A-bulbs and perhaps an R-30 flood, an R-30 spot, and a PAR-38 (the narrowest beam).

ENTRIES / **A bright welcome to the house**

Entries should be warmly lighted, enticing guests to come further inside. Effective fixtures range from the eye-catching and exciting to the simple and functional. They can set the house's lighting style.

Because entries often join hallways or stairs, give careful consideration to lighting for safety. Wall or ceiling fixtures can be placed to guide guests into the traffic pattern.

A light for the coat closet and one near a mirror for that last-minute check make entry lighting complete.

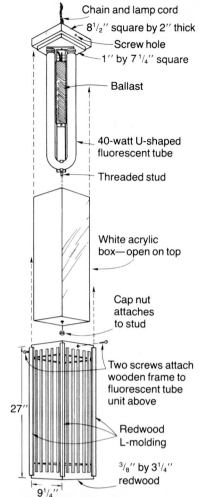

- Chain and lamp cord
- $8^1/_2''$ square by 2'' thick
- Screw hole
- 1'' by $7^1/_4''$ square
- Ballast
- 40-watt U-shaped fluorescent tube
- Threaded stud
- White acrylic box—open on top
- Cap nut attaches to stud
- Two screws attach wooden frame to fluorescent tube unit above
- Redwood L-molding
- 27''
- $^3/_8''$ by $3^1/_4''$ redwood
- $9^1/_4''$

Light on three levels

Suspended from the two-story-high ceiling, these redwood-trimmed rectangular lanterns light the balcony passage above as well as the entry below. Constructed by the homeowner according to the drawing at right, the wood trim and acrylic diffusing boxes warm the light emitted by the U-shaped fluorescent tubes within. Architect: Kenneth Lim.

Spotlighting the entry

Low-voltage track fixtures and attractive displays draw visitors into this entry gallery. Two VNSP (very narrow spot) MR-16 bulbs are trained on the vase and credenza; floods and more spots alternate down the hallway. Power comes to each fixture through a mono-point—a short length of track. Lighting design: Epifanio Juarez Design.

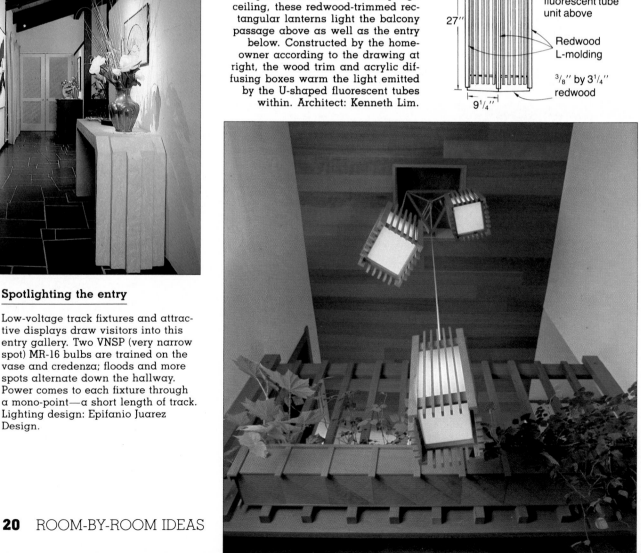

Lines of light lead you inside

Guiding visitors into the house, these semirecessed
fluorescent fixtures are fitted with reflectors and disk
baffles that direct the light upward, where it bounces
off the walls and ceiling for an airy, open feeling.
Architects: MLTW Turnbull Associates. Lighting design:
Richard Peters.

Providing light for an active family's needs in living rooms and family rooms can be a challenge. You'll want to include *task* lighting for reading, games, or handiwork, as well as *accent* lighting on artwork or architectural features. Low levels of *ambient* (general) light set a congenial mood for entertaining or watching television.

Dimmers and three-way bulbs in lamps make fixtures do double duty—the highest level serves as task light, and the lowest provides ambient light.

Lights focused on artwork or bookshelves provide both ambient light and a type of accent lighting. Valances, cornices, and baffles are effective ambient sources, too.

Starlight and downlights

Star-gazing may be great from this living room, but there are interesting indoor lights as well. Adjustable low-voltage downlights beam down from the ceiling and the soffit; the painting is washed by hidden spotlights. Incandescent strip lights add a warm glow to each display shelf. Lighting design: Donald Maxcy.

Fixtures on the move

Whether you're rearranging the furniture or moving to the opposite coast, these halogen fixtures can follow you. The torchère's built-in dimmer can match your moods—from up-tempo partying to late-night champagne and Stravinsky. On the right is a mini-reflector spotlight with a red filter; a second mini-reflector illuminates the brick backdrop from the side. When it's time for reading, the adjustable task lamp provides a powerful halogen punch. Fixtures courtesy of The Minimal Space.

Candlelight and a view

This picture window not only frames a beautiful harbor view but is also quite dramatic in its own right. The decorative candles are actually "lit" from above by two MR-16 spotlights on a dimmer. Ceiling accents come from two uplight cans—one behind the wood stove, the other behind the leather chair. A halogen floor lamp furnishes pinpoint task lighting. Lighting design: Peggy Kass.

Blending old and new

Recessed in ceiling bays, a row of modern wall washers creates attractive light patterns on a wall illuminated by antique wall fixtures fitted with delicate, flame-shaped bulbs. Table lamps and additional wall fixtures flanking the fireplace complete the picture. When the exterior lights are on (see page 73), an additional glow enters through the arched window at the left. Interior design: Marlene Grant and Margaret Shroeder/The Whitney Corporation.

A touch of brass

Two sleek torchères lend the warm look of brass to this cozy fireplace scene. Uplighting emphasizes the curved ceiling and textured plaster while providing most of the ambient light in the room. No electrical cords are visible; instead, cords run to plug-in outlets recessed in the floor directly below each fixture. Interior design: Sharon Kasser, Distinctive Interiors.

Twin lamps lend their light

A "popped-out" window brightens this room by catching daylight on three sides. At night, the window area is illuminated by two hand-crafted lamps sitting on a ledge be-hind the couch. The lamp bases, made from a pair of etched clay pots, were finished with rounds of clear pine (see drawing below). Pots and pine were then treated with a sealant for a low-gloss finish.

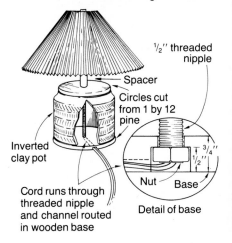

Spacer

½" threaded nipple

Circles cut from 1 by 12 pine

Inverted clay pot

¾"
½"

Nut   Base

Detail of base

Cord runs through threaded nipple and channel routed in wooden base

Color and light dramatize the decor

Vases, pillows, and bowls throughout this cream-toned room seem to vibrate with color, thanks to illumination with colored light that strengthens their own hues. In addition to low-voltage track fixtures, which supply accent lighting, an uplight under the plant creates giant shadows and the brass reading lamp provides task lighting. On the floor, a glowing globe adds interest. Half-bowl wall fixtures in the window corners send light up to the ceiling, and a splash of red from a track fixture floats above the city lights beyond. Lighting design: Randall Whitehead. Interior design: Christian Wright.

Subtle light source

Simple in design, this display pedestal gently illuminates the statue of Saint Francis, accenting its graceful lines and creating a halo of light on the wall behind it. The box was made of pressboard, covered with fabric, and topped with acrylic, as the illustration below shows. Three vent holes in the rear allow heat from the bulb to escape. Design: Marc Miyasato.

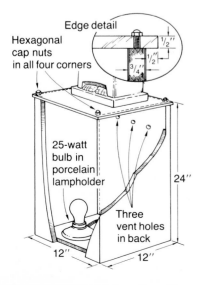

Edge detail

Hexagonal cap nuts in all four corners

1/2″
1/2″
3/4″

25-watt bulb in porcelain lampholder

24″

Three vent holes in back

12″   12″

Neon—a novel notion

A simple rectangle of white neon is used both to accent the architectural lines of this niche and to light it when it serves as a display stage. Tracks for glass shelves have been built in along either side to accommodate another type of display. Architect: Ted Tanaka.

**For special effect:
Antique Chinese jar
made into a modern lamp**

This table lamp holds a position of
importance in the room at right, adding a dash of bright color as well as
light. The lamp was professionally
made from an antique porcelain jar;
a dark wooden cap and base were
added as finishing touches. Design:
Ruth Soforenko Associates.

Downplayed fixtures set the scene

Open, recessed downlights on dimmers create versatile
general lighting in this room, where the fixtures them-
selves go bvirtually unnoticed. The overhang above the
fireplace hides a short segment of track, which holds a
spotlight for each painting. The jar lamp adds a well-
placed task light, while a spotlight above it accents the
plant. Behind the oriental screen in the background is
another downlight, generating a soft, ambient glow.
Interior design: Ruth Soforenko Associates.

Fireplace focal point

The addition of a light in the niche above this fireplace gives depth and focus to a subtle layering of structural curves and arches. The echoing curves of the smoky coral piece are dramatized by the sidelighting provided by a simple tubular bulb (see drawing below). Architect: Pamela M. Seifert.

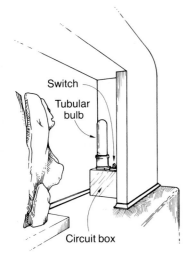

Switch

Tubular bulb

Circuit box

Art lighting illuminates room

Spanning the width of the room, this enameled cylinder houses a series of fluorescent tubes. A special reflector, shown in the detail below, directs the light onto the white wall—which, in turn, reflects a gentle light throughout the room. The ringed baffle cuts glare and lends a rosy tint to the light. Architects: MLTW Turnbull Associates. Lighting design: Richard Peters.

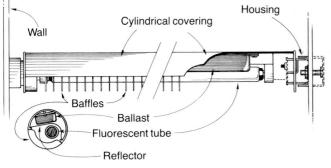

Wall

Cylindrical covering

Housing

Baffles

Ballast

Fluorescent tube

Reflector

Championship lighting

If someone misses a crucial pool shot in this bright, plush-carpeted alcove, it won't be because of glare or shadows. Three recessed downlights with glare-cutting black baffles spotlight the field of action; additional downlights wash the posts and fill in the background. In the adjacent family room, track fixtures light up artwork. Architect: Barry Fernald.

Brightening a wet bar

Ready for entertaining, this perky family room wet bar includes a built-in downlight to make serving easier. If the light's left on with the shutters closed, it provides an interesting ambient light as it peeps through the shutter cracks. Interior design: Ruth Soforenko Associates.

Bracket spills light above and below

Wrapping around the wall, this built-in wooden bracket washes both books and collectibles in an even layer of indirect light. The wooden facing hides fluorescent tubes and eliminates glare; at the same time, it becomes a decorative motif in its own right.

A study in understatement

The soft glow of indirect lighting complements the muted tones and textures of the furnishings in this corner sitting area. Built in behind the seating unit, as shown in the drawing below, fluorescent fixtures bathe the area in a particularly subtle kind of light. Interior design: Nancy Glenn.

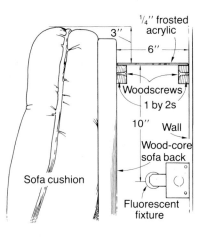

Sofa cushion

¼″ frosted acrylic

3″

6″

Woodscrews

1 by 2s

10″   Wall

Wood-core sofa back

Fluorescent fixture

Elegant or informal, your dining area benefits from careful lighting. Sparkling light from a chandelier, a pendant fixture, or downlights, combined with soft, indirect light on the walls and candles on the table, helps put your guests in a relaxed mood.

The main focus of dining room lighting should be the dining table, but a separate set of fixtures over your buffet supplies useful as well as ambient light at mealtimes.

Dimmers can be a real plus—turned up high, the light aids in the task of setting the table; on low, the gentle beam creates a festive atmosphere.

In order to dispel harsh shadows, augment downlights or pendant lamps over the table with light on the ceiling or walls.

The spotlight's on fine dining

A trio of spotlights mounted on a beam sets the stage for a fine dining experience. One fixture is aimed directly on the table; two more bounce light off the ceiling. All three are controlled by a dimmer. Above the cabinets, fluorescent tubes create a wash of indirect light, playing up the rough wall texture and backlighting the baskets. MR-16 spots brighten the pass-through area at left. Architect: Cliff May.

Low voltage, high drama

Easily adjusted low-voltage track fixtures in this dining area keep a low profile but pack a big punch. One halogen bulb pinpoints the table, two more light the vibrant painting. Each track has its own dimmer switch, visible to the left of the painting. A few steps beyond lies the kitchen, lit completely by low-voltage downlights. Slot apertures allow fine-tuning of the light for both task and accenting needs. Design: The Minimal Space.

Plenty of accent light—without glare

Lit precisely by tightly focused recessed downlights, this mirrored dining room has very dramatic light but no glare. Custom adjustable lenses, further controlled by glare-cutting pinhole apertures, aim low-voltage MR-16 bulbs. The framed mirror's carving is highlighted by one standard fixture and a second, lensless ("hard") bulb from nearby. Lighting design: Donald Maxcy.

Day or night, there's plenty of light

By day, this antique dining table is bathed in the same sunlight as the adjacent garden. After dark, brass nautical lanterns take up the task, filling the alcove with intimate reflected light and illuminating the path outside. Architect: J. Allen Sayles.

Halogen for a houseboat

A simple, spare halogen pendant fixture lights the dining table in this space-intensive houseboat. The fixture can be raised or lowered as necessary, and a dimmer adds even more control. In the kitchen, dimmed incandescent strip lights over the counter lend a soft, low-voltage ambience; when turned up full, they provide effective task lighting for culinary pursuits. Lighting design: Peggy Kass.

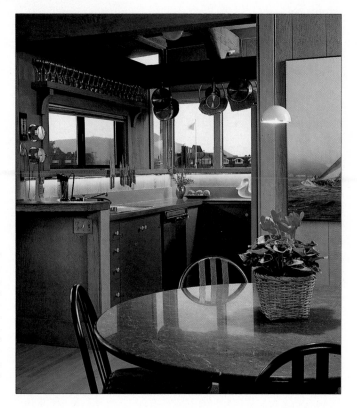

Tiny lights twinkle between diners and sky

In this owner-designed solarium addition, tubes of low-voltage mini-lights are fastened to ceiling beams; two strips of molding nailed along either side of the tubes give a finished look. Along the original eave line runs a row of eyeball recessed lights—the most versatile fixtures available that would fit into the narrow space between ceiling and roof. Design: Steven Osburn. Interior design: Barbara Wolfe Interiors.

Glassware display and easy serving at a bright buffet

This European modular buffet unit was fitted with lights to accent glassware and illuminate the serving area. Tucked behind the faceboard at the top of each glass case, mini-tracks with tubular incandescent bulbs light all the shelves. Four small recessed downlights over the buffet hold 25-watt reflector bulbs. Both sets of lights are on dimmers, to provide an ambient glow when attention is focused on the table. A convenient plug-in outlet was also added at the right corner of the serving area. Design: Stanford Electric Works and Eurodesign Ltd.

Sconce that's stunning in its simplicity

A half-bowl sconce accents the texture of reed wallpaper while providing ambient light for a gracious dining atmosphere. To achieve a feathery silhouette, an uplight can fixture is aimed at the wall from behind the plant. Interior design: Design Times Two.

A subtle quartet to dine by

Four deeply recessed downlights complement the oak furnishings in this clean-cut setting. With 50-watt PAR bulbs, fixtures on dimmers offer a wide range of levels, from bright light when used alone, as shown, to a subtle suggestion of light in combination with candles on the table. Inside the fixtures, metallic coating directs light in a controlled beam and cuts glare. On the left side of the ceiling, two recessed low-voltage downlights are visible. They send light to accent artwork (not pictured) on a wall. Architect: Jack Woodson. Lighting design: James Cooper. Interior design: Design Professionals Incorporated.

Informal fixture combination

A combination of fluorescent and incandescent light makes this informal dining area inviting. A trough that supports fluorescent fixtures (see drawing below) runs the length of the room, bracketed to the wall at either end. Each fixture serves a definite purpose: the trough contributes a gentle, general light, and the pendant lamp directs its light onto the table-top. Because both fixtures are opaque, they create no reflection on the undraped glass doors.

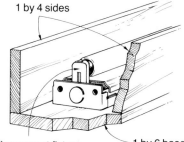

1 by 4 sides

Fluorescent fixture   1 by 6 base

Uncomplicated counter idea

For casual eating, a pass-through counter at the corner of this kitchen is illuminated with square recessed lights. These inconspicuous fixtures brighten the area without complicating its open lines or competing with the basket display. Cream-colored tiles reflect light from above, as well as that from the kitchen. Interior design: Ruth Soforenko Associates.

Often a gathering place, the kitchen benefits from general lighting for after-hours snacks or entertaining. And whether one cook is at work or you have a crew of kitchen helpers, task lighting over the sink and on the countertops and rangetop is essential.

You'll want strong, shadowless light right over each kitchen work area. In most cases, shielded strip lights under the cabinets are best to light the counter area, while direct downlights illuminate the sink and work islands. Light-colored countertops and walls add brightness, because they reflect light.

If your countertops are well lighted, general illumination on the ceiling or walls need only be bright enough to ensure safe movement about the room. Whether you choose decorative or functional fixtures, remember that, because they're in the kitchen, you'll need to clean them often.

Putting light in its proper place

Everything in this small kitchen is in perfect order, including the precisely placed track lighting. Low-voltage fixtures with MR-16 bulbs spotlight the microwave, the cooktop, a vase of flowers, and even the wall clock. The fixtures can be easily swiveled and rotated for exact placement; most bulbs are fitted with accessory baffles for an even tighter focus. Interior design: The Minimal Space.

Fluorescents and incandescents team up

Color-corrected (2,700°K) PL fluorescent downlights in the ceiling produce plenty of ambient and task light in this kitchen. An incandescent fixture in the vent hood shines down on the cooktop. R-30 incandescent downlights in the window soffit and glass display case (see detail at right) provide accents and a soothing light level when used alone. Lighting design: Epifanio Juarez Design.

All the lighting is indirect

This kitchen's indirect lighting is subtle, shadow-free, and efficient. Fluorescent fixtures are standard industrial side-mounted strips, hidden by valances; each fixture is mounted near the front of the shelf or cabinet to bounce maximum light off the white tiles. The "incandescent" fluorescent (I/F) tubes produce a pleasing color cast and work well with the other light sources in the house. Tubes adjacent to work surfaces are housed in clear protective jackets. Architect: Peter C. Rodi, Designbank.

At last—attractive fluorescent fixtures

These wall-mounted fluorescent bar fixtures cast even
light both up and down, reflecting ambient light off walls,
ceiling, and cabinets. Task and accent lighting are provided by recessed halogen downlights. Fluorescent undercabinet fixtures complete the picture. Lighting design:
Ross De Alessi/Luminae, Inc.

Curving brick conceals sink downlights

In this handsome renovation of an older home, rich, dark colors in the lower portion of a south-facing stained-glass window serve to cut down glare during the day. At night, two recessed downlights installed behind a brick cornice (shown in the drawing below) bathe the sink area with light. Design: Design Times Two.

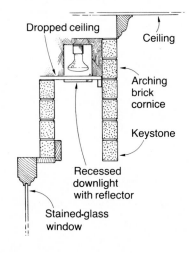

Dropped ceiling

Ceiling

Arching brick cornice

Keystone

Recessed downlight with reflector

Stained-glass window

Well-lighted "garage"

Here's a perfect example of light where it's needed. In this appliance garage, the slim fluorescent fixture—not visible when viewed from normal standing height—spreads its crisp light over the area where the appliances are used. The wall at the back is painted white for good reflective quality. Interior design: Nancy Glenn.

Skylight at center stage

Bright and cheery, with light where it's needed and wanted, this kitchen features an artificially illuminated skylight for a soft, diffused glow after the sun goes down (see drawing at left below). Countertop lighting comes from slim undercabinet fluorescent fixtures, while the sink counter receives light from glass-covered, easy-to-clean recessed fixtures. Architects: Michael D. Moyer and Lyle Mosher. Interior design: Janet Wasson Interiors.

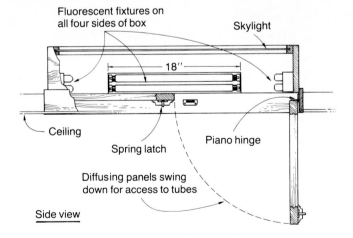

Fluorescent fixtures on all four sides of box

Skylight

18"

Ceiling

Piano hinge

Spring latch

Diffusing panels swing down for access to tubes

Side view

Reflection upon reflection

Cherry red lacquered cabinets reflect and repeat the double neon rectangles used to provide low general light and high visual interest in this kitchen. Plenty of strong task light for the countertops comes from slim fluorescent fixtures under the cabinets. A convenient series of electrical outlets on a strip has been built in at the back of the counter and disguised with a matching lacquered veneer.
Lighting design: Luminae, Inc.
Interior design: Nancy Glenn.

Polished product of a household handyman

This handsome brass-bound butcher-block shelf serves three purposes—beautifully. It acts as a display platform for a collection of shiny cookware and green plants while supporting lighting fixtures and hiding the necessary wiring. Brass fixtures adjust to illuminate cooktop or countertop. As shown in the drawing below, wires originating in the ceiling run down through the brass pole and then through a channel routed in the butcher block's top. This arrangement eliminates unsightly wires that might interfere with items displayed on top.

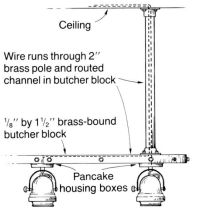

Ceiling

Wire runs through 2" brass pole and routed channel in butcher block

$\frac{1}{8}$" by 1$\frac{1}{2}$" brass-bound butcher block

Pancake housing boxes

Bright points spark a basket display shelf

Ambient light for informal kitchen gatherings can be provided by a shelf lighted like this. As the drawing at right shows, a plug-in strip or a parallel conductor strip fitted with nightlight fixtures can do a tidy job. Design: Bruce Velick.

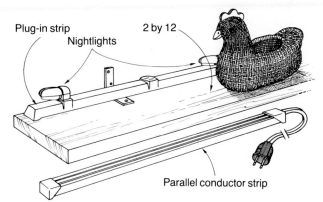

Plug-in strip

Nightlights

2 by 12

Parallel conductor strip

Whether your work area is a sewing room, a woodshop, or a drafting table, you'll need enough light to see easily—and you'll want to place the light carefully, so that your work surface is free from shadows. With a combination of general lighting and adjustable task lighting, you can avoid strong contrasts between a specific work area and the rest of a room.

If your surroundings have a high reflectancy, task areas will be easier to light: light-colored blotters on dark-finished desks and light-hued walls above workbenches or sewing tables reflect light back onto the work area.

Fluorescent built-ins and downlights are best for ambient lighting; a PL fluorescent or halogen task lamp is good for close work.

Lighting sets a quiet mood

Incandescent strip lights, mounted in a continuous cove above cabinets and windows, suffuse this office ceiling with soft indirect light; MR-16 downlights with pinhole apertures illuminate the desk and chairs. A wall sconce fills in the corner. Interior design: Barbara Jones Light. Lighting design: Susan Huey/Luminae, Inc.

Open, bright, and ready for writing

The crisp lines of this desk area, where everything's within easy reach, are conducive to getting things done. A long fluorescent fixture fills the whole white desktop area with worklight. Above, three small recessed downlights illuminate the bookshelves' contents and add a softer incandescent tone to the work area. Architect: David Jeremiah Hurley.

A studied lighting scheme

In this handsome study, designed for nighttime bookkeeping, strong task light falls onto the desktop from the recessed downlight above. Two more downlights are stepped back on either side to light the file drawers when they're opened. A series of wall-washer fixtures illuminate the bookshelves and add to the room's overall light level. Lighting design: Luminae, Inc.

Ceiling grid creates a soft, even light

There's no reason why office lighting can't be both effective and fun to look at. This custom-designed ceiling grid was installed along with the light fixtures. General lighting comes from a standard fluorescent ceiling panel; accent light on the wall is from three pendant fixtures that extend from a track above the grid. Design: Ruth Soforenko Associates.

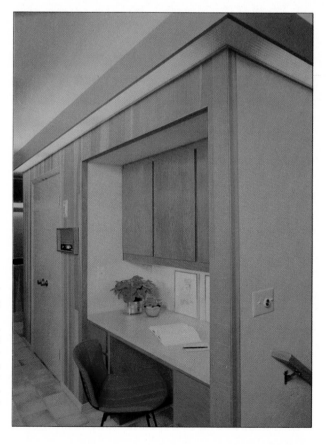

Built-in lighting for a built-in desk

Neatly tucked into an alcove, this kitchen desk is flooded with task light by an undercabinet fixture installed above the white desktop. A wall bracket, which traces the perimeter of the room, spreads light down on the warm cedar paneling as well as upward to the ceiling. Architect: Kenneth J. Abler.

Low overhead

A garden view, bright white surfaces, and effective light-ing help make this converted basement office a cheery, productive work space. Glass pendant fixtures follow the L-shaped work counters, and a shiny chrome lamp boosts task lighting at the drafting board. Interior design: Gail Woolaway & Associates.

Soy-tub ceiling fixtures

For a homeowner whose hobby is making wine, this wine cellar definitely ranks as an essential work area. Handmade recessed downlights are made (as shown in the drawing below) from soy tubs, cut in half and treated on the inside with a high-gloss finish to reflect light. Each one has a 325-watt globe bulb for a good measure of general light. Additional fixtures, hidden behind the ceiling beams and wired with dimmers, spread an indirect glow over the wine racks.

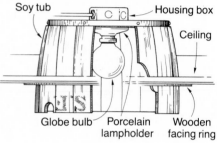

Soy tub   Housing box   Ceiling

Globe bulb   Porcelain lampholder   Wooden facing ring

Shadowless sewing and laundry light

An expanse of white countertop stands ready for even the most ambitious sewing project. A 10-foot-long fluorescent tube hidden under the shelf floods the work surface with shadowless task light. Just a few steps away, the laundry area is also outfitted with fluorescent fixtures. Architect: David Jeremiah Hurley.

Basement workshop under lights

Sunny yellow pendant lamps with 100-watt bulbs provide color as well as overlapping circles of strong, concentrated task light in this basement shop. Recessed fixtures with wide beams spread a high level of general light through the room for less demanding activities.

With a full staircase—or even just two steps down to another level—it's important to provide adequate light for safety. The nose or edge of each tread and the depth of each step should be clearly defined. One of the best ways to achieve this is to combine a direct downlight fixture over the stairs (to light the edges) with a softer light projected from the landing below (to define the depth of the stairs). In choosing and placing fixtures, be sure they won't direct any blinding glare into the eyes of people anywhere along the stairway.

Another option in lighting stairs is to build low-voltage fixtures into the wall just above every third or fourth step. Lights hidden in a handrail are also an unobtrusive but effective way to light the tops of stair treads.

See page 57 for a look at an entry hallway with well-lighted stairs.

Low-voltage lights climb the stairs

Glowing mini-lights on a remote transformer light the display niche in the foreground, while an MR-16 fixture on a mono-point illuminates the stair-side niche. Adjustable halogen downlights (not visible in photo) wash the walls, and tiny aisle lights beside the stair treads keep climbers on course. Design: Epifanio Juarez Design.

From ship to shore

As shown above, low-voltage marine lights, designed for rough treatment in boats and buses, define every other stair tread. The open staircase gets its general light from the high-ceilinged living room. Architect: David Petta. Lighting design: David Malman.

Mini-lights outline each step

Plushly carpeted stair treads seem to float on layers of light that provide both a clear view of the edge of each tread and precise perception of the depth of each step. The cross section below shows how quarter-round molding nailed to each stair nose shields the low-voltage mini-lights. Risers were painted white and left uncarpeted to allow light to spill out. To avoid dimming due to voltage drops, each line of lights connects directly to the transformer. Lighting design: Randall Whitehead and Bart Smyth.

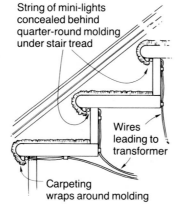

String of mini-lights concealed behind quarter-round molding under stair tread

Wires leading to transformer

Carpeting wraps around molding

Unobtrusive, energy-saving wall panels

Easy to add in new construction, this type of illuminated plate fixture does its job safely and unobtrusively. Using minimal energy, the low panels can be left on all night to provide enough light for safe navigation. They may be the perfect solution for a short stairway between two house levels. Architect: J. Alexander Riley.

Light at your fingertips

For a compact, efficient solution to stair lighting, a fluorescent tube is hidden behind a slim handrail. Fluorescent tubes are well suited to this use—they don't produce much heat, so there's no danger of getting burned. Architect: David Jeremiah Hurley.

Hallways can be slim passage-ways, inviting galleries, or even open, glassed-in spaces. But as routes for human traffic, they should be neither much dimmer nor much brighter than adjoining rooms, so that your eyes don't have to make radical adjustments when you're going from room to room.

For safety, switches to control the lights should be at both ends of a hall. Ceiling or wall fixtures can aim light onto the walls or floor without getting in the way, even in the narrowest hallway. You'll want to provide light for any closets along a hall, either from inside or by directing a ceiling fixture at the door.

Lights wash paintings and passageway

This hallway could be a long, dim tunnel. Instead, it doubles as a well-lit art gallery, inviting guests to browse awhile before passing through. Paintings along the way are illuminated by a skylight during the day and by 120-volt track fixtures once night falls. Design: Peter C. Rodi, Designbank.

Extension into adjacent hallway

A sense of architectural continuity arises here from the long fluorescent tube fixture that seems to extend through the wall from the family room into the adjacent hallway. The two separate tube fixtures have a special reflector like the one on page 29, producing a high, even light level. The hall glows with brightness as light is distributed further by white walls. Architects: MLTW/Turnbull Associates. Lighting design: Richard Peters.

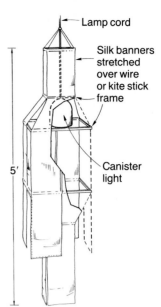

Lamp cord

Silk banners
stretched
over wire
or kite stick
frame

5′

Canister
light

Lanterns lead the way

Sun-filled by day, this hallway is lighted for a soft nighttime look. Pairs of wall fixtures illuminate the floor and
steps, and send a glow of light upward. A pinhole aperture spotlight high on the wall highlights the trailing
plant. Two custom-made kite lanterns (see drawing above,
at right) sway gracefully as they fill the hall with light.
Architect: Charles Moore. Lighting design: Richard Peters.
Lantern design: Charles Moore and Christina Beebe.

Angled tracks follow the maze

A mazelike passage full of angles
posed a real problem in this older
house. A line of track lights, broken
into lengths to complement the
angles, makes a handsome solution.
Aimed at each painting and doorway
along the way, fixtures provide all the
light that's needed. Interior design:
Jane Simons.

Bedroom lighting requirements range from the subtlest to the brightest. On the subtle end of the scale, soft levels create a quiet aura. Bright—but separate and adjustable—reading lights on either side of a double bed allow one person to sleep while the other reads into the wee hours.

A switch by the bed to turn off the main room light is handy.

You may want to include a light in front of a full length mirror, but remember: the light should shine on the person, not on the mirror. Lights in front of the bureau and inside closets aid in clothes selection.

His and her lights

Dimmable plaster wall sconces provide a soft wash of up-lighting, bringing out the pastels in this elegant bedroom design. Each partner also has a built-in MR-16 downlight, controlled by a dimmer switch on each side; slot-aperture trims help aim the lights, making certain that one bedmate won't be disturbed by the other's late-night reading. Lighting design: Epifanio Juarez Design.

Inviting light to relax by

Lighted by recessed downlights, the window seat in this bedroom extends an invitation to relax awhile. Open recessed downlights in a larger size illuminate the closets and bureau area for ease in clothing selection. Thanks to dimmers, both sets of lights produce a broad range of light levels—for atmosphere or activity. Lighting design: Luminae, Inc.

The warm glow of wood

Incandescent lighting makes this open bedroom arrangement seem more cozy. Track fixtures play up the artwork
and the paneling's warm tones; the bedside lamp creates
a soft pool of light for reading or relaxing. Overhead,
golden uplighting paints the roof beams. Architect:
William Arthur Patrick.

Reading lamps built into the headboard

Warm scallops of light from inside this freestanding headboard stand in for separate reading lamps. In the dressing area beyond, recessed downlights illuminate grooming activities. Architect: Phoebe Wall.

Built-in eyeballs light bedside alcove

Custom European-style cabinetry frames a well-lighted headboard and alcove. Eyeball downlights with incandescent bulbs provide most of the light; they're controlled by dimmers built into the headboard. The brass reading lamps have dimmable switches, too. Design: Ruth Soforenko Associates.

Indirect lights for a relaxing atmosphere

Dramatic indirect lighting creates a relaxing atmosphere in this bedroom. A strip of low-voltage mini-lights tacked underneath outline the bed-frame and send a glow of light onto the hardwood floor. The rice paper screen diffuses soft blue light from a spotlight with a blue filter. Another uplight glows behind the pillar, while the shimmer of the globe light at the window is reflected on the warm-toned wooden chest. Lighting design: Randall Whitehead.

Designed for a teenager's private domain

Planned with a teen-age daughter in mind, this bedroom serves as a cozy place for record playing, chatting with friends, and reading textbooks, as well as sleeping. A wall bracket built into the shelf unit houses a series of tubular incandescent bulbs. The light level on these can be dialed with a dimmer, from atmospheric low to industrious high. A brass lamp with a milky shade and adjustable base provides good reading light at the head of the bed. Interior design: Barbara Wolfe Interiors.

Shedding light on the sartorial subject

On the subject of dressing, these two deeply recessed ceiling fixtures take a clear stand. Their wide beams reach into the closets to help in selecting clothes and provide plenty of glare-free light for a final check of attire in the full-length mirror. Architect: David Jeremiah Hurley. Interior design: Jill Chozen.

Clearly illuminated closet

Lighting the way to easy clothing selection is a small track unit mounted high above the door in this orderly closet. Fitted with small fluorescent fixtures that burn cool and don't use much energy, the fixture is controlled by a switch on the outside of the closet. Architect: David Jeremiah Hurley.

BATHROOMS / **Clearly lighted reflections**

The trick to lighting bathrooms is to provide task light that's gently flattering and yet strong enough for grooming. Lights around a mirror used for shaving or putting on make-up should spread light over a person's face rather than onto the mirror surface. To avoid heavy shadows, it's best to place mirror lights at the sides, rather than only at the top of the bathroom mirror.

Consider dimmers here, too, to tone down the light level when it's not needed. In larger bathrooms, a separate fixture to light the shower or bath area and perhaps one for reading may be appreciated. And plan low-energy night lighting for safety, convenience, and decorative accent.

Light and shadow

Three types of recessed downlights provide this bathroom's dramatic accents, yet supply plenty of general illumination as well. Open downlights with black baffles and incandescent bulbs light the sink area; eyeball fixtures wash the opposite wall, and low-voltage MR-16s with slot apertures create the scalloped design behind the tub. A pair of heat lamps play their part, too. Interior design: Ruth Soforenko Associates.

A shining example

Low-voltage downlights, filtered sunlight, and wall mirrors work their magic in this small tub area. The mirrors reflect the fixtures many times over, but there's no glare: slot apertures help focus each MR-16 bulb. Two downlights illuminate the flowers behind the tub; additional fixtures (visible in the mirrors) shine straight down. Lighting design: Donald Maxcy.

Sparkling lines of mirror lights

Lines of low-voltage mini-lights set between mirror panels add sparkle and highlight the unusual angles of this bathroom. At night, with the other lights off, the tiny points of light provide a whimsical form of night-light. Recessed ceiling fixtures placed over the tub and each sink provide good overall lighting. Note the eyeball fixture trained on the painting in the reflection. Design: Design Times Two.

The shape of elegance

The graceful curve of this bathtub is accentuated by the linear tile design on the side—and further underscored by the discreet lighting below. The secret? A string of low-voltage minilights tucked up behind the tub overhang. Design: Dagmar Thiel, Kitchen and Bath Design.

Bright bars beside mirrors

Straightforward in design, light sources line up at the sides of these mirrors. Sidelighting is the most flattering and effective way to provide light at a grooming or make-up mirror. Though these incandescent tube fixtures are of European manufacture, similar fixtures made to operate on U.S. current are available. Architect: William Stout.

Soffit lights the scene below

Mullioned soffit lighting in the bath is in keeping with the window trim in this remodeled older home. Fluorescent tubes mounted on the ceiling above the diffusing acrylic spread a strong, even light over the counter. The mirrored walls, often used with this type of soffit lighting, stretch the light further through reflection. Architects: Michael D. Moyer and Lyle Mosher. Interior design: Janet Wasson Interiors.

Up and down light

Doing double duty, a soffit variation adds height to this bathroom's cedar ceiling as it provides the mirror area with good, shadowless grooming light. The drawing at right shows the two separately operated sets of lights. Architect: Kenneth J. Abler.

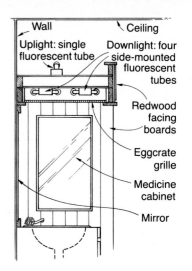

Wall   Ceiling

Uplight: single fluorescent tube

Downlight: four side-mounted fluorescent tubes

Redwood facing boards

Eggcrate grille

Medicine cabinet

Mirror

Walls of light

This L-shaped bathroom benefits from vertical rows of incandescent bulbs flanking the vanity, as well as a curved wall of glass blocks. Decorative clear globe fixtures visible in the mirror help light the shower area. Architect: William B. Remick.

A bright bath just for kids

Perimeter fluorescent strip lighting and four centrally located downlights keep things lively in this windowless bathroom built for kids. White tile and wall-wide mirrors help spread the light. Architect: Douglas Kahn.

Luminous countertop creates low-key lighting

A luminous cultured onyx vanity countertop doubles as a unique, effective nightlight. Four 18-inch, 40-watt fluorescent tube fixtures—good choices because of their cool, energy-efficient light—were secured inside the cabinet (see drawing at right). The designer chose cultured onyx because the fluorescent light's color reacted with some other countertop materials to produce an unattractive color tone. Design: Design Times Two.

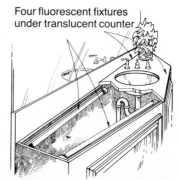

Four fluorescent fixtures under translucent counter

Space-age line and color

Dazzling imported tile, stylized pedestal sink, and bright lighting combine to create this uncompromisingly modern guest bath. Strong beams from recessed downlights and twin mirror-mounted fixtures put light right where it's needed most. Architect: Weston Whitfield.

It's all done with mirrors

Mirror trickery in this small bath makes it seem spacious by reflecting light both from the fixtures and from the white surfaces. Open ceiling fixtures, deeply recessed to avoid glare, provide most of the room's illumination. The low-wattage clear globe bulbs at either side of the mirror add enough light to soften any shadows from the downlights. Interior design: Nancy Glenn.

Theatrical bulbs star, with fluorescent tubes in a supporting role

Two sets of lights are at work here. For applying make-up, theatrical incandescent bulbs surrounding the mirror shed a flattering radiance on the face. Meanwhile, fluorescent tubes, hidden behind the wall bracket that extends around the room, spread a wash of light up to the ceiling and down over the paneled walls. Architect: Kenneth Lim.

Safety, security, and decoration—all three are functions of outdoor lighting, and all can be achieved with a good lighting scheme. The only rule is to keep both glare and wattage at a low level.

At the front door, recessed downlights or an indirect wash from accent lights work well. If the entry is well lit, you won't need to flood the front walk, but you will want to light steps, changes in direction, and any dark corners or dense shrubbery.

At night the view outside ends where the light ends. Balance light levels on both sides of a picture window to reduce unwanted reflections. Use soft light in the foreground, build up the middle ground, and save the highest wattage for the background.

Low-voltage fixtures are especially good for subtle accenting effects and glare control. Many can also be picked up and repositioned. But when it comes to security needs or to uplighting a large oak, 120 volts is still your best choice.

Dimmers on multiple circuits help you paint a landscape to match your mood. All switches should be centrally located indoors. Timers, remote controls, and daylight-sensitive photocells are all helpful devices.

From any angle, it's inviting

Twin iron fixtures atop stone pillars announce this well-lit front entry; each globe houses three 120-volt, 25-watt bulbs. Low-voltage swan's-neck spread lights define the garden borders and illuminate the front walk; well lights accent the trees and add a feeling of depth to the garden. At the doorway, recessed downlights create a bright wash of light. Landscape design: Rogers Gardens/Colorscape.

Arches glow inside and out

This stylish front entry emits golden light, thanks to effective indoor and outdoor lighting. An antique chandelier in the front hall glistens through the doorway's leaded-glass arch and sidelights. Outdoors, recessed incandescent downlights wash the living room window; two more downlights beckon visitors to the front door. A flush-mounted stair fixture helps lead the way. Interior design: Marlene Grant and Margaret Shroeder/The Whitney Corporation.

Window announces the front door

This front entry was treated like an interior—note the accented display alcove on the left. One lidded wall washer highlights the alcove; another lights the door. Inside, a recessed fixture shines through the leaded-glass window. Architect: Kip Stewart. Lighting design: Donald Maxcy.

Downlights lead the way

Most pathways are lit from ground level; here, the cobblestone walk is spotlighted from above. A 7½-watt incandescent wall fixture announces the house; eave-mounted downlights with PAR-36 spots light the flower boxes, walkway, brick wall, front steps, and front porch. Stained-glass upstairs windows, lit from within, add a warm glow. Lighting design: Susan Huey/Luminae, Inc.

Outdoor lighting extends the indoors

The view at night used to stop at the sliding glass doors.
Now, eave-mounted MR-16 downlights paint the courtyard
patio; a PAR-36 fixture lights the garden pool from within.
Movable MR-16 uplights spotlight the hanging baskets
and tree, and more uplights paint the plantings along
the fence in the background. Lighting design: Epifanio
Juarez Design.

Pillar lights built from wood

Simple but striking, these custom-
made entry fixtures house weatherproof sockets and A-bulbs; louvers
aim light down to prevent glare. Beyond the gate, pathway and accent
lighting draws visitors into the tiled
courtyard. Landscape architects:
Fry + Stone Associates.

Gargoyles guard the pool

These spotlighted statues boldly
define the edge of the pool—and
provide a dramatic foreground for
the sparkling city lights beyond. Each
head is lit by its own 150-watt framing
projector, mounted across from the
pool area. Garden palms—one for
each statue—are accented by low-
voltage uplights concealed behind the
low tiled wall. Landscape design:
G. Grisamore, Inc.

Lights up

This garden lighting design extends
outdoor living well into the evening. A
pair of dimmer-controlled pool lights,
with a twinkling border of mini-lights
to mark the step, gives gentle, overall
illumination. Low-voltage uplights
accent the pyracanthas on the left.
The trees in the large bed at the rear
have their own lights. Landscape
architects: Stone & Fischer.

Reflections on outdoor lighting

Good lighting makes this house a
sight to behold—both inside and out.
A built-in underwater light sets the
pool aglow; spread lights and uplights
bring the pathways and garden to life.
Wall-mounted fixtures mark the steps,
leading to the spacious, well-lit
veranda. Landscape architect: Peter
Wright Shaw Associates, Inc. Garden
lighting: Arbor Electrical Co.

Tiled spa takes center stage

This garden fountain plays a dual role as a heated spa:
the underwater pool light can be dimmed for a relaxing
soak. Low-voltage PAR-36 uplights highlight the palm
trees; other fixtures splash light on the birds of paradise.
Landscape architects: Fry + Stone Associates.

Indirect pathway lighting: a closeup

In this detail of the courtyard lighting shown on page 75, low-voltage mini-lights recessed behind the tile cap of the seat wall provide soft illumination. Light bouncing off the stucco and shiny outdoor pavers increases the effect. Landscape architects: Fry + Stone Associates.

Hanging lanterns glow from below

These elegant lanterns were designed for candlepower; with the addition of custom-fitted lenses and electrical wiring, they've found a new life in the garden. Uplighting, provided by hidden low-voltage well lights, seems to emanate from the lanterns as well. Design: Ross De Alessi/Luminae, Inc.

Secret garden

Twin wall fixtures, custom-built from redwood, flank the passage into this storybook garden. Matching path lights, half-hidden by the border hedge, march into the distance. Design: Bob Waterman.

Bright but cozy garden corner

Path lights following the curving brick border beam low-voltage light onto massed flowers. At the end of the line, a soothing spa beckons. A concealed uplight highlights the tree branches above the scene. Landscape design: Rogers Gardens/Colorscape.

WIRING IT ALL TOGETHER

MATERIALS • TOOLS • TECHNIQUES

Here's an array of lighting materials and tools—from tiny wirenuts to lengthy tracks. Installation techniques are explained on the following pages.

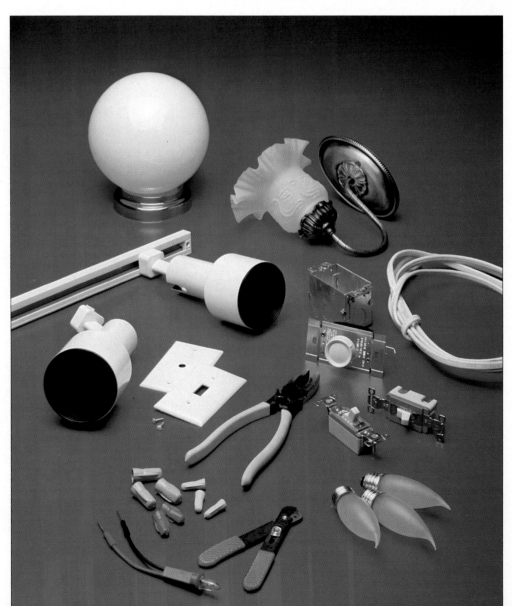

Once you've analyzed your lighting needs and learned about the various bulbs, tubes, fixtures, and controls available, you're ready for the next step: improving the lighting in your home. Whether you plan simply to replace an ON-OFF switch with a dimmer or to enhance an entire room with new fixtures, many of the how-to-do-it basics are the same.

This chapter will show you how to determine how much light (measured in watts) you can safely add to existing circuits, how to work with wire and other materials, and how to install fixtures, plug-in outlets, switches, and outdoor lights. If you need to do more than tap into existing circuits, consult the *Sunset* book *Basic Home Wiring*, or call in a licensed electrician.

Should you do your own work?

Doing your own electrical work may not always be the best idea. Your local building department may restrict how much and what kinds of new wiring a homeowner may undertake. If yours is an older home, for instance, and you discover that the wiring inside the walls is the old-fashioned knob-and-tube variety (see page 84), local regulations may require that new hook-ups be made by a licensed electrician.

Even if your locality doesn't restrict what kinds of electrical work you do in your own home, you may still wish to use the services of an electrician. If electrical problems crop up that you don't understand—or if there's any doubt in your mind about how to proceed with a home lighting project—it's best to call on a professional.

Codes & permits

If you want to do your own hook-ups, you should first talk with your building department's electrical inspector about local codes, the National Electrical Code, and your jurisdiction's requirements concerning permits and inspections.

The National Electrical Code spells out the wiring methods and materials to be used in all electrical work. The Code forms the basis for all regulations applied to electrical installations, and its central purpose is safety.

The information given in this book complies with guidelines set out by the National Electrical Code. Some cities, counties, and states amend the Code to suit their particular purposes, though, and as a result, specific regulations can vary from county to county and even from town to town.

Safety first

The most important rule for all do-it-yourself electricians is this: *never work on any electrically "live" circuit, fixture, plug-in outlet, or switch*. Your life may depend on it.

Before starting any work, you must disconnect the circuit you'll be working on at its source, either in the service entrance panel or in a separate subpanel. If your circuits are protected by fuses, simply removing the appropriate fuse will disconnect the circuit from incoming current. In a service entrance panel or subpanel equipped with circuit breakers, you can disconnect a circuit by switching its breaker to the OFF position.

To make sure that you disconnect the correct circuit, turn on a light somewhere along the circuit before you remove the fuse or turn off the circuit breaker. The light will go out when you've removed

the correct fuse or turned off the correct breaker.

If you have any doubt about which fuse or breaker affects which circuit, shut off *all* current coming into your home at the main disconnect (identified as MAIN). Usually the main disconnect is located at the service entrance panel, as shown below.

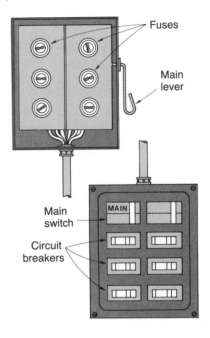

So that no one will come along and replace the fuse or reset the circuit breaker while you're working, tape a note to the panel that explains what you're doing. Then either carry the removed fuse with you in your pocket or tape the appropriate circuit breaker securely in the OFF position.

WIRE COLOR-CODING

For simplicity's sake, unless otherwise indicated the wires shown in this book are color-coded as follows:
- Hot wires—thick black or red
- Neutral wires—thick white
- Grounding wires—narrow black

Actual wires come in a greater variety of colors. Here are some of the wire or wire insulation colors you may come across:
- Hot wires—usually black or red, but may be any color other than white, gray, or green. (If a hot wire is white, it should be taped or painted black near terminals and splices for proper identification.)
- Neutral wires—white or gray
- Grounding wires—bare copper or aluminum, or green. (Grounding wires are rarely black.)

CIRCUITRY CONSIDERATIONS

The word "circuit" refers to the course an electric current travels, from the source of power (the service entrance panel or a subpanel wired to it) through some device using electricity (such as a light fixture) and back to its starting point, the source. What may appear to be a hopelessly tangled maze of wires running through the walls and ceilings of your home is actually a well-organized system composed of several circuits.

How your home is wired

Today, most homes have what's called three-wire service. The power company connects three wires to the service entrance panel. Each of two "hot" wires supplies electricity at 120 volts. During normal operation, the third wire, a neutral wire, is maintained at zero volts.

Three-wire service provides both 120-volt and 240-volt capabilities. One hot wire and the neutral wire can be used to complete a circuit for 120-volt needs, such as lights and plug-in outlets. Both hot wires can be used to complete a circuit for 240-volt needs, such as an electric range or clothes dryer.

Many older homes have only two-wire service, with one hot wire at 120 volts and one neutral wire. Two-wire service doesn't have 240-volt capability.

Service entrance panel. The control center for your electrical service is the service entrance panel. Housed in a cabinet or box, it's often located outside your home, below the electric meter. It can also be on an inside wall, directly behind the meter.

In this panel you'll usually find the main disconnect (the main fuses or main circuit breaker), the fuses or circuit breakers protecting each individual circuit, and the grounding connection for your entire system.

Circuit distribution center. After passing through the main disconnect, each hot wire connects to

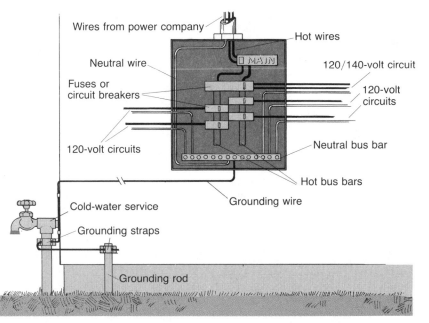

one of two strips of metal, called "bus" bars, in the distribution center. These bars accept the amount of current permitted by the main fuses or circuit breaker, and divide that current into smaller units for the branch circuits, as shown above. The neutral wire runs directly to its own bus bar. The distribution center may be housed in the service entrance panel or in a subpanel located elsewhere in the home.

Circuits for lights. In most homes, several light fixtures and plug-in outlets operate on the same circuit by what is called parallel wiring, as shown below. The hot and neutral wires run continuously from one fixture or outlet box to another.

(see pages 92–93) are installed along the hot wire to control individual lights or groups of lights.

Grounding to prevent shock. The National Electrical Code requires that every circuit have a grounding system. Grounding ensures that all metal parts of your home's wiring system will be maintained at zero voltage, for all are connected directly to the earth. In the event of a short circuit, a grounding wire carries current back to the circuit distribution center—rather than through the body of a person who comes in contact with the faulty circuit—and ensures that the fuse or circuit breaker will open, shutting off the flow of current (see drawing below).

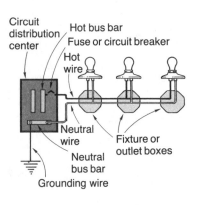

Wires or plug-in cords branch off from these continuous hot and neutral wires to individual light fixtures. Switches and dimmers

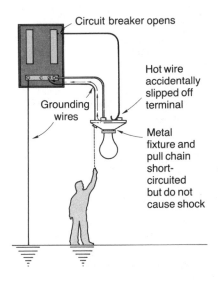

The nonmetallic sheathed cable (see page 84) used to tap into most circuits carries its own grounding wire. The grounding connection from a housing box to a plug-in outlet (see page 91) is made with a short piece of wire (called a jumper) screwed to the box. The screws that hold a metal fixture to its box ground the fixture (see page 88)—except with a hanging fixture, in which case a separate grounding wire is run from box to fixture.

Mapping your circuits

If you plan to install additional lighting in your home (as opposed to simply replacing fixtures), it's important to know which circuits control which existing appliances, fixtures, plug-in outlets, and switches. Some of these circuits may already be carrying the maximum current allowed by law (to calculate wattage, see at right).

To decode your wiring, start by giving a number to each fuse or circuit breaker in the circuit distribution center (if you have more than one subpanel, be sure to number all branch circuits). Next, draw a map showing every room in your home, including the basement and garage. Using the symbols shown in the sample map below, indicate on your own map the approximate location of each appliance, fixture, plug-in outlet, and switch.

To chart the circuits, you'll need a small table lamp or night light that you can easily carry around with you to test all plug-in outlets. After turning the first circuit breaker to the OFF position or removing the first fuse, go through the house and check all appliances, switches, and plug-in outlets; on your map, label those that are now dead with the circuit number.

Repeat the process with each circuit, first making sure that you've turned the previous circuit breaker back on or replaced the previous fuse.

Calculating maximum watts

Once you've mapped your circuits, plan to add fixtures or plug-in outlets to those circuits controlled by 15-amp circuit breakers or fuses; adding lights to circuits that can carry more than 15 amps is often illegal.

As a rule a 15-amp circuit can handle a maximum of 1,440 watts. Add up the watts marked on the appliances and bulbs fed by the circuit you want to add to. The difference between this sum and 1,440 is the total number of watts that you can add to the circuit.

If you're confused by load calculations or if you want to know if you can tap into a circuit rated at more than 15 amps, call on your building department's electrical inspector. Take along your circuit map, a list of the appliances and bulbs currently serviced by the circuit in question, and a second list of the fixtures and outlets you'd like to add.

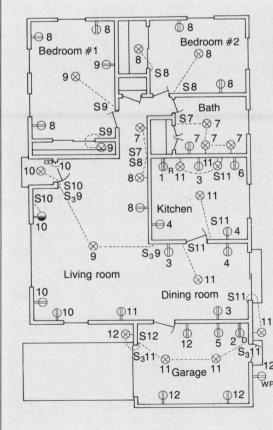

CIRCUIT MAPPING

At left is a circuit map of a typical two-bedroom house. Note that the dashed lines indicate which switch controls which fixture; they do not show wire routes.

Electrical symbols	Circuit identification
⊗ Light fixture	1. Range (50 amp)
⊖ Double plug-in outlet	2. Dryer (30 amp)
⊖ Double plug-in outlet, half controlled by switch	3. Kitchen and dining room (20 amp)
S Single-pole switch	4. Kitchen and dining room (20 amp)
S₃ Three-way switch (two switches control one fixture)	5. Washer (20 amp)
	6. Dishwasher (20 amp)
⊕R Range outlet	7. Bath and hall (15 amp)
⊕D Dryer outlet	8. Bedroom #2 (15 amp)
⊡ Doorbell	9. Bedroom #1 (15 amp)
⊖WP Weatherproof plug-in outlet	10. Living room (15 amp)
	11. Living room (15 amp)
----- Switch wiring	12. Garage (20 amp)

WORKING WITH WIRE

With only a few tools and materials, and the knack of making splices, you can handle most wiring chores yourself.

Some useful tools

In addition to such common tools as standard and Phillips screwdrivers and needle-nose pliers, the following specialized tools come in handy for doing electrical work.

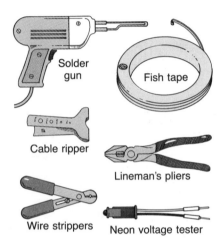

Lineman's pliers are an electrician's basic tool. Serrated jaws hold wires firmly, and just behind the jaws is a set of wire cutters.

Wire strippers are available in several designs, ranging from a simple two-piece scissors type to a complex self-clamping type.

A cable ripper rips the outer insulating sheath on nonmetallic sheathed cable, allowing you to peel away the insulation. Use this tool only on standard flat two-wire cable.

Fish tape is a big help whenever you're going to pull wires through walls (see page 86). Made from long pieces of flattened spring steel, 25- and 50-foot fish tapes come on reels for easy handling. For short distances, you can use a straightened coat hanger or a piece of #12 wire with one end bent into a hook.

A neon voltage tester determines which is the hot wire in a two-wire

circuit with ground. You touch one probe to the grounding wire (or metal box) and the other probe to the other two wires, one at a time. The tester lights when the second probe contacts the hot wire. CAUTION: Because a circuit must be left on for testing, keep your fingers off the probes' bare metal tips when using a voltage tester.

A solder gun is needed only for splicing tie-ins to old knob-and-tube wiring (see "Splicing," at right); solder guns can be rented.

Basic materials

At most, you'll need only three types of materials—nonmetallic sheathed cable, wirenuts, and housing boxes for wirenut splices—to complete most interior wiring chores. Before you purchase any materials, be sure they conform to the requirements of your local building code.

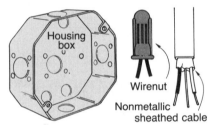

Nonmetallic sheathed cable (type NM) contains one or two hot wires (usually wrapped in black or red thermoplastic), a neutral wire (wrapped in white thermoplastic), and usually a grounding wire (bare or wrapped in green thermoplastic). To ensure the best splices, use only cable containing all-copper wire, not aluminum or copper-clad aluminum wire.

Wirenuts join and protect the stripped ends of spliced wires within housing boxes. Once you know how many wires of what size you'll be splicing together, you can get wirenuts in the proper sizes.

Housing boxes provide connection points inside walls or ceilings, either for splicing wires or for mounting light fixtures, switches, or plug-in outlets. Boxes are either metal or plastic. Metal boxes are stronger, but unlike plastic ones, they require grounding.

Rectangular boxes that hold only switches or plug-in outlets are called switch boxes. Outlet boxes are used to mount light fixtures. For more details on housing boxes, see pages 85 and 87.

Splicing—easier than you think

Most wire splices are made in housing boxes with wirenuts. If you discover that your home is equipped with old-fashioned knob-and-tube wiring (separate hot and neutral wires threaded through porcelain knobs and tubes), you may need to use a 250-watt solder gun. Both wirenut and soldered splices are discussed below.

Wirenut splices are easy to make. Start by stripping off an inch of insulation from the ends of the wires you're going to join. Hold the stripped ends together, twist them clockwise 1½ turns, and snip off ⅜ to ½ inch from the wires so that the ends are even. Finish by screwing the wirenut on clockwise.

Soldered splices (copper to copper only) are required to carry current from hot and neutral knob-and-tube wires into a housing box, as shown below.

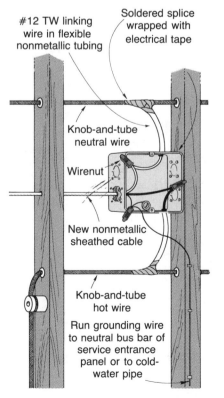

#12 TW linking wire in flexible nonmetallic tubing

Soldered splice wrapped with electrical tape

Knob-and-tube neutral wire

Wirenut

New nonmetallic sheathed cable

Knob-and-tube hot wire

Run grounding wire to neutral bus bar of service entrance panel or to cold-water pipe

Strip 2 inches of insulation from the knob-and-tube wire you want to splice, and 1½ inches from the end of the linking wire. Sand the wire ends until shiny with coarse-grained emery paper. Twist the bare end of the linking wire tightly around the bare knob-and-tube wire, forming a coil ¾ inch long, and snip off the stub end of the linking wire.

Heat the coil with a 250-watt solder gun; then touch the tip of a roll of rosin-core solder to the coil. You'll know that the coil has reached the proper temperature when the solder flows readily into the spaces within the coil and does not flow out again. Once the spaces are filled, take away the gun and the roll of solder.

When the liquefied solder has rehardened and the coil is cool, wrap the coil and the bare portion of the knob-and-tube wire with rubber insulation tape; seal the tape by wrapping it in the opposite direction with electrical tape.

EXTENDING AN EXISTING CIRCUIT

Your lighting project may call for adding a new fixture, switch, or plug-in outlet to an already existing circuit. In this section we present techniques for extending a circuit with nonmetallic sheathed cable (type NM). When you're ready to connect your new device, turn to pages 88–93.

Selecting a power source

A circuit can be tapped wherever there's an accessible outlet, switch, fixture, or junction box. The only exceptions are when you have a switch box without a neutral wire or when there's a switch-controlled fixture at the end of a circuit.

Because of code restrictions, however, you must tap the correct *type* of circuit. And you must determine that the circuit doesn't already carry the maximum electrical load allowed. For help, see "Mapping your circuits," page 83.

Before deciding where to tap the circuit, consider how you'll route wire to the new fixture, switch, or plug-in outlet. Examine your home's construction, looking for the easiest paths behind walls, above ceilings, and under floors.

The box tapped must be large enough to accommodate the new wires and must have a knockout hole through which you can thread the new cable. If the source is accessible but the box isn't right, replace it.

CAUTION: Before working on any existing box or device, disconnect the proper circuit by removing the fuse or switching the circuit breaker to OFF.

Preparing for new boxes

After selecting the power source but before routing the cable, you must buy the right boxes, determine where to put them, and cut holes for them in the walls or in the ceiling.

Choosing boxes. For switches and outlets and for fixtures that weigh 24 ounces or less, consider cut-in or plain boxes, which can be secured in the spaces between studs or joists. For heavier fixtures, use boxes that can be anchored to studs or joists.

Many recessed fixtures come prewired to their own housing boxes. For more about these, see page 89.

Selecting a box location. To locate a box in a wall or ceiling, you'll need to locate the positions not only of studs and joists but also of any obstructions, such as pipes or wires. CAUTION: Before you do any work, be sure to shut off power to all circuits that might be wired behind the wall or ceiling.

Drill a small test hole where you want the box. Then bend a 9-inch length of stiff wire to a 90° angle at the center, push one end of the wire through the hole, and turn it. If it bumps into something, move over a few inches and try again until you find an empty space.

When locating a box on a plaster-and-lath wall, chip away enough plaster around the test hole to expose a full width of lath. Plan to center the box on the lath.

Cutting the hole. Trace the box's outline on the wall or ceiling (see below), omitting any protruding brackets from your outline.

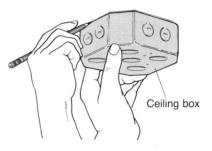

Ceiling box

To cut the box hole, drill pilot holes in the corners of the outline; then, with a keyhole saw or saber saw, cut along the outline. If you're cutting through plaster, first apply masking tape to the outside border of your outline to prevent the plaster from cracking. Brace a plaster ceiling as you cut.

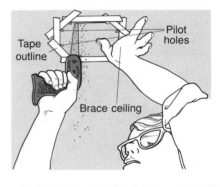

Pilot holes

Tape outline

Brace ceiling

Routing cable

After cutting a hole but before mounting the box, you must run cable from the power source to each new box location. Access from an unfinished basement, an unfloored attic, or an adjacent garage can make your work much easier. Getting cable into walls, ceilings, or floors that have coverings on both sides requires some special tricks.

Routing cable where there's access. Where you have access from a basement or crawlspace or from an attic, plan to run cable along joists or beams, or through holes drilled in them. From these areas you can "fish" cable through walls that are covered on both sides.

After cutting the box hole, drill a small guide hole down through the floor or up through the ceiling to mark the location. Then, from the basement or attic, drill a ¾-inch hole next to your guide hole up through the sole plate or down through the top plates (see below).

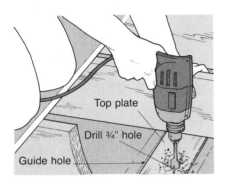

Top plate

Drill ¾" hole

Guide hole

To make sure your path is clear, have a helper hold a flashlight in the box hole while you peer through the drilled hole. If you can't see the light beam, a fire block or some other obstruction is in the way. Either drill through the block or cut away the wall covering and notch the block.

If your access is from below, run fish tape or #12 wire in through the box hole and down through the drilled hole. Strip the cable's end to bare wires, twist them around the fish tape or wire, and wrap with tape; then draw the cable back through the box hole.

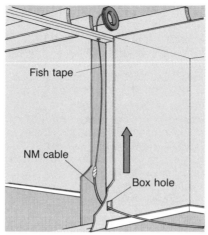

Fish tape

NM cable

Box hole

When working from above, first run tape down to the box hole; then secure the cable to the tape and pull it back up, as shown above.

Running cable where there's no access. If you don't have access, you'll probably need to cut away some wall, ceiling, or floor coverings. Wallboard is relatively easy to cut away and replace. But some other materials, such as ceramic tile or some types of plaster, are more difficult to patch and should be left alone when possible.

The drawing at right shows one way to route wire to a new light fixture and switch where there's no easy access. Remember that cable installed less than 1¼ inches from a finished surface

should be protected by a ¹⁄₁₆-inch metal plate where the cable passes through wood.

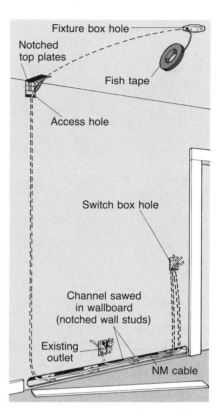

Fixture box hole

Notched top plates

Fish tape

Access hole

Switch box hole

Channel sawed in wallboard (notched wall studs)

Existing outlet

NM cable

What if ceiling joists run perpendicular to your route? Look upstairs: access may simply be a matter of removing a small section of the subfloor.

SURFACE WIRING

Where routing wire through walls is difficult and cutting open walls, ceilings, and floors is not feasible, metal raceway provides an alternative. Self-grounding tubes snap into clips that have been screwed or bolted to the wall or ceiling. Two #14 TW wires are then threaded through the tubes.

Standard outlets, fixtures, and switches are attached to raceway wires in the same way that they're attached to in-the-wall wiring (though without the grounding wire), but they must be housed in extension boxes.

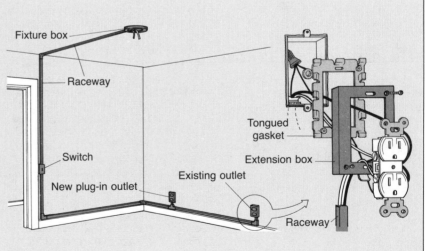

Fixture box

Raceway

Switch

New plug-in outlet

Existing outlet

Tongued gasket

Extension box

Raceway

Mounting new boxes

Before you mount a new housing box, remove a knockout for each new cable. NM cable must be secured to a metal box either with built-in cable clamps or with a separate metal cable connector. Cable need not be clamped to a nonmetallic box if the cable is stapled within 8 inches of the box; if you can't staple, choose a box with built-in clamps. Always leave 6 to 8 inches of cable extending into the box for making connections.

How you mount the new box will depend on its type. Several examples are shown in the drawing at right.

Cut-in box. Once this box is mounted, it can't be removed, so try out the fit—without the metal spring ears—and have the cables in place before you install it. Tighten the screw at the back of the box.

Plain box. This box is a good choice for plaster-and-lath walls: simply clear away enough plaster to accommodate the ears and then screw the box to the lath. If necessary, adjust the ears to bring the box flush with the wall.

Box with flange. From above or behind, check the fit of the box in the hole; then nail or screw the flange to the side of the joist or stud.

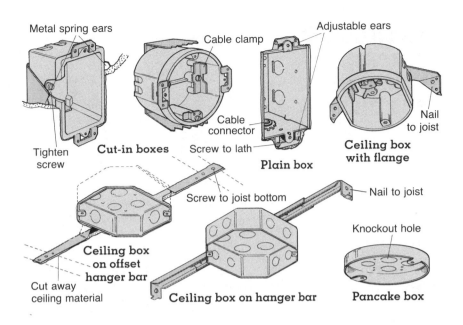

Metal spring ears
Tighten screw
Cut-in boxes
Cable clamp
Cable connector
Screw to lath
Adjustable ears
Nail to joist
Plain box
Ceiling box with flange

Cut away ceiling material
Ceiling box on offset hanger bar
Screw to joist bottom
Nail to joist
Knockout hole
Ceiling box on hanger bar
Pancake box

Ceiling box on offset hanger bar. This box works well where you don't have access from above. Trace the hanger's outline on the ceiling material, remove this strip, and screw the hanger to the bottoms of two joists.

Ceiling box on hanger bar. The hanger bar for this type of ceiling box is installed from above. Adjust the hanger's width; then nail or screw it to the sides of two joists.

Pancake box. Simply screw this box to the bottom of a joist or hang it from a hanger bar.

Tapping into the circuit

You can tap power at a fixture, outlet, or switch box, as shown below. A fourth option is a junction box, where wires are simply joined.

First, disconnect the proper circuit by removing the fuse or switching the circuit breaker to OFF. Then peel back the outer sheath from the new cable and cut off the sheath and any separation materials. To strip the insulation off the wires and splice them to the old wires, see page 84.

Fixture box as power source

From circuit distribution center
Grounding wires
To existing switch
Hot wires (white wire should be painted black near splice)
Neutral wires
To new boxes

Outlet box as power source

From circuit distribution center
Hot wires
Neutral wires
Grounding wires
To new boxes

Switch box as power source

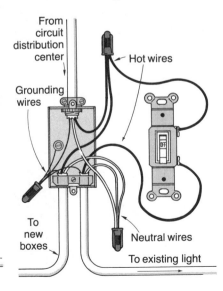

From circuit distribution center
Hot wires
Grounding wires
To new boxes
Neutral wires
To existing light

INSTALLING SURFACE-MOUNTED FIXTURES

Surface-mounted fixtures are either attached directly to a housing box or suspended from the box by a cord, chain, or pole.

The size and weight of the new fixture determine the mounting method: many ceiling and wall fixtures can be screwed directly to the box's ears. Heavier fixtures, however, may require fastening to the box with a mounting bar, hickey, or reducing nut; any fixture that weighs over 50 pounds must be secured to a joist or beam as well as to the box. New fixtures usually come with their own mounting hardware, which is adaptable to any standard fixture box.

Grounding metal fixtures. The National Electrical Code requires that all incandescent and fluorescent fixtures with exposed metal parts be grounded.

If the fixture box itself is grounded, the nipple or screws holding the fixture to the box will ground the fixture. There's one exception: a fixture suspended from a cord, chain, or pole needs a grounding wire run from the socket to the box. Most new fixtures are prewired with a grounding wire.

If the fixture box is not grounded (as is the case when your present house wiring includes no grounding wire), you'll have to extend a grounding wire from the box to the nearest cold-water pipe. To do this, you'll need a length of bare #12 copper wire, a grounding strap, and enough patience to route the wire so that it won't be an eyesore. Wrap one end of the wire around the grounding screw or around the nipple or screw holding the fixture to the box; secure the other end to the screw that holds the strap to the pipe.

Replacing a fixture. Whether you're replacing an old fixture with one of the same type or with a different kind, the steps are the same.

First, disconnect the circuit by removing the fuse or switching the circuit breaker to OFF. Carefully remove the glass cover, if any,

from the old fixture. Unscrew the canopy from the fixture box; detach the mounting bar if there is one. Have a helper hold the fixture to keep it from falling.

Now, make a sketch of how the wires are connected. If they're spliced with wirenuts, unscrew them and untwist the wires. If the wires are spliced only with electrical tape, simply unwind the tape. New splices will be covered with wirenuts. Lay the old fixture aside.

Strip ½ inch of insulation from the new fixture's wires. Then, as your helper holds up the new fixture, match its wires to the old wires as shown in your sketch. Splice with wirenuts (see page 84).

Secure the new fixture by reversing the steps you took to remove the original, using any new hardware included with the fixture.

Adding a new fixture. Installing a new surface-mounted fixture is much like replacing one, once the cable has been routed from a power source and the fixture box and switch installed. Before doing any work, be sure the power to the circuit has been disconnected.

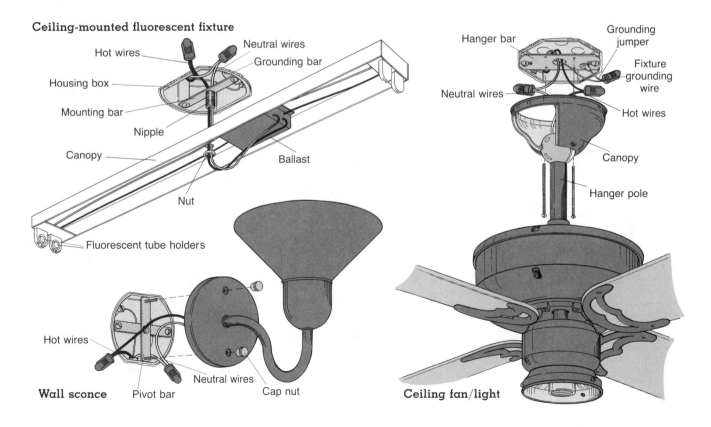

Ceiling-mounted fluorescent fixture

Hot wires · Neutral wires · Grounding bar · Housing box · Mounting bar · Nipple · Canopy · Ballast · Nut · Fluorescent tube holders

Hanger bar · Grounding jumper · Fixture grounding wire · Neutral wires · Hot wires · Canopy · Hanger pole

Wall sconce · Hot wires · Neutral wires · Pivot bar · Cap nut · **Ceiling fan/light**

New nonmetallic cable routed to the box should include a grounding wire, which is attached to the box's grounding screw. If more than one cable enters the box (for example, a separate cable may be connected to the switch box), you'll need to attach the end of a grounding jumper (a short length of #12 wire) to the grounding screw and splice its other end to the ends of the grounding wires in the cables. Cap the splice with a wirenut.

One cable

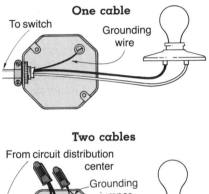

To switch

Grounding wire

Two cables

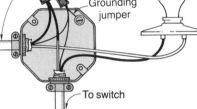

From circuit distribution center

Grounding jumper

To switch

If you've chosen a nonmetallic box for your fixture, it doesn't need grounding, but you'll have to ground the fixture. Look for a box with a metal grounding bar (see drawing at far left, facing page). If the fixture is at the end of the circuit, attach the cable grounding wire to the bar. If the fixture is in the middle of the circuit, make a grounding jumper to join the cable grounding wire to the bar.

To install the fixture, match the box's wires to those of the fixture— black wire to fixture hot wire, white wire to fixture neutral wire. If the fixture has a separate grounding wire, join it to the grounding wires in the box. Cap all splices with wirenuts. Mount the fixture with the hardware specified by the manufacturer.

Note: If the fixture is heavy, have a helper hold it while you work; or hang it from the box with a hook made from a wire coat hanger.

ADDING RECESSED DOWNLIGHTS

There are two basic types of recessed downlights: one comes pre-wired and grounded to its own housing box; the other must be wired into a junction box attached to a joist.

Recessed fixtures need several inches of clearance above the finished ceiling, so they're most easily installed below an unfinished attic or crawlspace. Because of the heat generated by many types of downlights, you must remove insulation within 3 inches of the fixture and make sure that no combustible materials are within ½ inch (with the exception of joists or other blocking used for support).

Most low-voltage downlights come with an integral transformer attached to the frame; if yours doesn't, you'll first need to mount an external transformer nearby and then route wire to the fixture.

Cutting the ceiling hole. Before installing the fixture, you'll need to cut a hole for the fixture housing in the ceiling between two joists. If there's no crawlspace above the joists, find the joists (and any obstructing wires or pipes) from below by the bent-wire method described on page 85; don't forget to shut off power to any circuits that might be wired behind the ceiling before drilling exploratory holes.

Once you've located a suitable place for the fixture housing, trace its outline on the ceiling with a pencil; use a keyhole saw or saber saw to cut the hole.

Downlight with box. With this type, the fixture and its box are premounted on a metal frame.

Downlights with adjustable hanger bars, such as the fixture shown above right, are easy to install from above: simply nail the ends of the bar to joists on either side; then clip the trim or baffle into place from below.

If you don't have access, look for a "remodeling" fixture. The version shown at right slips through the ceiling hole and clips onto the edge of the ceiling. The fixture

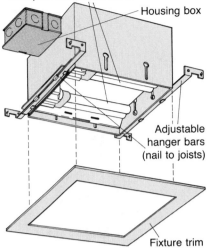

Compact fluorescent tubes

Housing box

Adjustable hanger bars (nail to joists)

Fixture trim

housing then snaps into the socket and frame. (Hook up the wires to the circuit *before* positioning the fixture and frame.)

Downlight without box. To connect this type of fixture to incoming cable, you must select a junction box that can be nailed to a joist, as

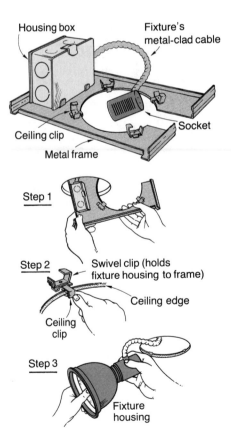

Housing box

Fixture's metal-clad cable

Ceiling clip

Socket

Metal frame

Step 1

Step 2

Swivel clip (holds fixture housing to frame)

Ceiling edge

Ceiling clip

Step 3

Fixture housing

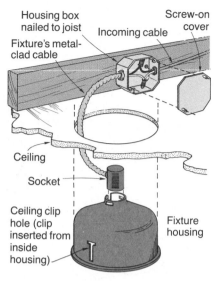

Housing box nailed to joist
Screw-on cover
Incoming cable
Fixture's metal-clad cable
Ceiling
Socket
Ceiling clip hole (clip inserted from inside housing)
Fixture housing

shown above. After clamping and wiring the fixture's cable into the junction box, snap the fixture housing into its socket. Then push the fixture into place and secure it to the ceiling material with clips. The metal-clad cable grounds the fixture to the box.

INSTALLING TRACK SYSTEMS

Track systems are mounted, either directly or with mounting clips, to the wall or ceiling. Power is provided by using either a wire-in or plug-in connector, as described below. Both types are shown at right. Tracks are often wired into two separate circuits controlled by two switches.

Low-voltage track fixtures with integral transformers or adapters can be plugged into a standard 120-volt track. Other systems require an external transformer to step down power to the track itself. In this case, you'll need to mount the transformer and then route wire to the track location. This method has one advantage: it cuts down the distracting "hum" produced by some low-voltage installations.

Attaching the connector. A plug-in connector, which includes a 12-foot cord and a lamp plug, lets you place a track wherever the cord

will reach an outlet. The connector is mounted flush against the wall or ceiling. Note that plug-in connectors are available only with single-circuit tracks.

A track system with a wire-in connector is hooked up directly to a housing box. Whether you use an existing box or install a new one, you'll need as many wall switches as your track has circuits. If you're simply replacing a fixture with a single-circuit track system, you can use the existing wall switch. By using a special connector available with some track systems, you can bring in power along a track run rather than at the end.

To install a wire-in connector, position the fixture box saddle and then splice the connector's wires to the incoming cable wires. Cap each splice with a wirenut. Some connectors attach to the fixture box cover; others are simply held in place by the track.

Mounting the track. When you attach a track directly or with mounting clips to the ceiling or wall, you'll use mounting screws or tog-

gle bolts in predrilled holes. To lay out and drill the necessary holes, line up a chalkline or the edge of a yardstick with the center line of the connector; snap or draw a line to the proposed end of the track.

Setting a length of track beside the line, mark the positions of the knockout holes in the roof of the track. These marks show you where to drill.

If you're using a plug-in connector, it will lie flush against the mounting surface so that you can attach the track directly to the wall or ceiling. Hold up the first length of track (you may need a helper), join the end to the connector, and secure the track to the ceiling or wall with mounting screws or toggle bolts. Attach the remaining lengths of track in the same way.

If you're using a wire-in connector, you may need special clips to hold the track 1/4 to 1/2 inch away from the mounting surface. Screw or bolt the clips to the ceiling or wall; then slip the first length of track onto the connector. Press it, and succeeding lengths, into the clips.

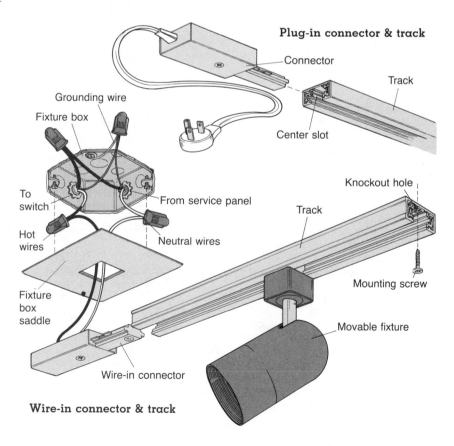

Plug-in connector & track
Connector
Track
Center slot

Grounding wire
Fixture box
To switch
Hot wires
From service panel
Neutral wires
Fixture box saddle
Wire-in connector

Knockout hole
Track
Mounting screw
Movable fixture

Wire-in connector & track

ADDING PLUG-IN OUTLETS

All new outlets for 15- or 20-amp circuits should be of the grounding type shown on this page. Outlets are rated for a specific amperage and voltage; be sure to buy the type you need.

Most outlets have three different-colored screw terminals. The brass ones are hot, the white or silver ones are neutral, and the green one is the grounding terminal. If your outlet is a backwired type, as shown below, the hot (black) and neutral (white) terminals will be identified; the grounding wire must still be attached to the green screw terminal.

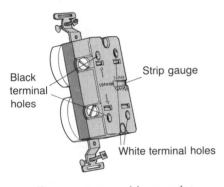

Black terminal holes

Strip gauge

White terminal holes

If you want to add an outlet to a circuit that doesn't have a grounding wire, you can either use a grounding type and run a separate grounding wire to a nearby cold-water pipe or, in some areas, substitute an old-style non-grounding outlet. To ground to the water pipe, use bare #12 copper wire and a grounding strap.

CAUTION: Before wiring any outlet, be sure to disconnect the circuit by removing the fuse or switching the circuit breaker to OFF.

The drawing below shows three common wiring situations. The first, the usual arrangement, is for several outlets to be wired in parallel, with all outlets always hot. In the second, the outlet is controlled by a wall switch. In the third, the two halves of the outlet operate independently of each other, with one half controlled by a switch and the other always hot. (In this case, use pliers to break off the ear that connects the outlet's two hot terminals.)

The drawings on this page assume your housing boxes are metal; if not, there's no need to ground the boxes, but you will have to attach a grounding wire to each outlet.

To wire an outlet, first join the circuit grounding wire or wires with a grounding jumper from the outlet; for a metal box, add a jumper from the box. Next, join the hot and neutral wires entering the box with the correct terminals on the outlet, adding jumpers as required; a typical installation is shown above, at right. Cap each splice with a wirenut.

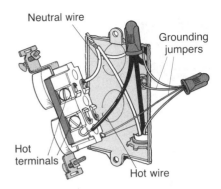

Neutral wire

Grounding jumpers

Hot terminals

Hot wire

After you've made the wire attachments, fold the wires back into the box and screw the outlet to the box. Adjust the screws in the mounting slots until the outlet is straight. If it isn't flush, shim it out, using the break-off portions of the outlet's plaster ears or some washers. Finally, add the cover plate.

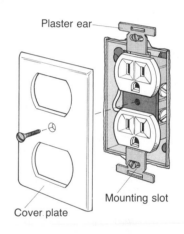

Plaster ear

Mounting slot

Cover plate

Both halves always hot

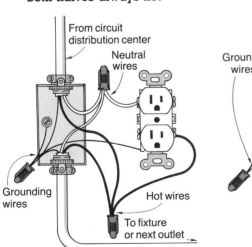

From circuit distribution center

Neutral wires

Grounding wires

Hot wires

To fixture or next outlet

Both halves controlled by wall switch

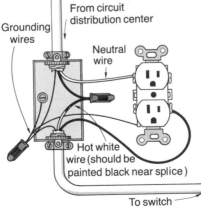

Grounding wires

From circuit distribution center

Neutral wire

Hot white wire (should be painted black near splice)

To switch

Bottom half always hot, top half controlled by wall switch

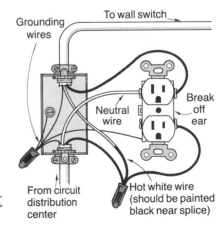

Grounding wires

To wall switch

Neutral wire

Break off ear

From circuit distribution center

Hot white wire (should be painted black near splice)

WIRING SWITCHES & DIMMERS

Most switches in a home are either single-pole or three-way. With a single-pole switch, one switch controls one or more light fixtures or plug-in outlets. With a three-way switch, two switches in different locations both control one or more fixtures or outlets.

A third type, the dimmer switch, not only allows you to fine-tune the light level, but also saves energy and bulbs.

A switch must have the same amp and voltage rating as the circuit you plan to tap into. If your home's wiring is aluminum, be sure that the switch is designed to be used with aluminum wire—if it is, it will be identified by the letters CU-AL. Remember when wiring that *switches are connected only to hot wires*.

The switches shown on these pages have no grounding wires because the plastic toggles used on most home switches are shock-proof. However, if switches are housed inside metal boxes, the *boxes* need to be grounded. When installing a nonmetallic switch box at the end of a circuit, secure the end of the grounding wire between the switch bracket and the mounting screw.

CAUTION: Before wiring any switch, be sure to disconnect the circuit by removing the fuse or switching the circuit breaker to OFF.

Wiring single-pole switches

Single-pole switches have two screw terminals of the same color (usually brass) for wire connections and a definite right-side-up orientation—you should be able to read the words "ON" and "OFF" embossed on the toggle. It makes no difference which hot wire goes to which terminal.

Because of cable-routing logistics, circuit wires may run from the circuit distribution center through the switch box to the light fixture

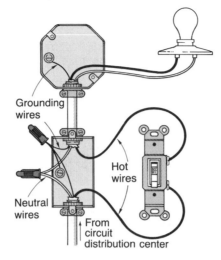

Single-pole switch wiring if power enters switch box

Grounding wires — Neutral wires — Hot wires — From circuit distribution center

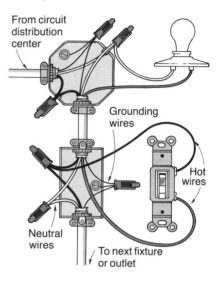

Single-pole switch wiring if power enters fixture box

From circuit distribution center — Grounding wires — Neutral wires — Hot wires — To next fixture or outlet

box, or to the light fixture box first, with a switch loop to the switch box. Both setups are shown above.

To wire a single-pole switch, first join the neutral (white) wires, if any, and cap the splice with a wirenut. Next, join the grounding wires and, for a metal box, add a grounding jumper. Finally, connect the hot wires to the switch's screw terminals.

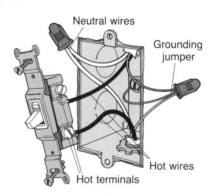

Neutral wires — Grounding jumper — Hot wires — Hot terminals

If your switch is the backwired type with push-in terminals, simply push the stripped hot wires into the terminal holes.

Once you've made the connections, fold the wires behind the switch and push the switch into the box. Screw the switch to the box, adjusting the screws until the switch is vertical. If the switch isn't

flush with the wall, use the break-off portions of the switch's plaster ears or some washers as shims. Finally, screw on the cover plate.

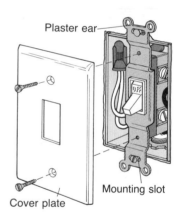

Plaster ear — Mounting slot — Cover plate

Wiring three-way switches

These switches have two screw terminals of the same color (brass or silver) and one of a darker color, identified by the word "common." Either end of a three-way switch can go up. It's important to observe, though, which terminal is the common one; it may be located differently from the drawings on the facing page. Circuit wires may run first either through the fixture box or through one switch box.

To wire a pair of three-way switches, first connect the hot wire

Three-way switch wiring if power enters fixture box

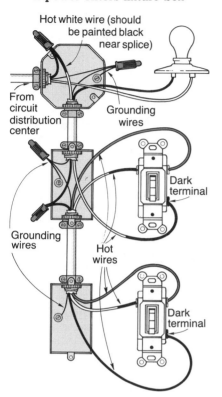

Hot white wire (should be painted black near splice)

From circuit distribution center

Grounding wires

Dark terminal

Grounding wires

Hot wires

Dark terminal

Three-way switch wiring if power enters switch box

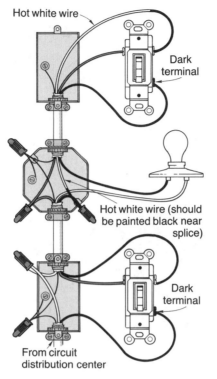

Hot white wire

Dark terminal

Hot white wire (should be painted black near splice)

Dark terminal

From circuit distribution center

Whether its purpose is to highlight plantings and structures, discourage prowlers, or light pathways and recreation areas, outdoor lighting is a welcome addition to any house. You can either extend your home's 120-volt system into the garden with a variety of permanently placed fixtures or step the system down to 12 volts with lighter-weight fixtures that can be easily moved.

If you're thinking of adding outdoor lights to an existing circuit, see "Calculating maximum watts," page 83. If you need to add a circuit, consult an electrician or refer to the *Sunset* book *Basic Home Wiring Illustrated*.

Electrically, there's no difference between wiring inside and outside. The materials you use, however, are different. Because outdoor wiring must survive the elements, materials are stronger and more corrosion resistant. Also, everything must fit exactly to prevent water from entering.

Adding a 120-volt system

To install a 120-volt outdoor system, you'll need a set of fixtures, outdoor housing boxes, and weatherproof 120-volt cable or conduit. You may also want to add an indoor switch and timer. You activate the system by tying into an existing power source.

Housing boxes. Outdoor boxes come in two types: so-called "driptight" boxes that seal vertically against falling water and "watertight" ones that seal against water coming from any direction. Unless you can ensure protection from rain, sprinklers, and even the garden hose, it's best to choose watertight boxes. Several types are shown on pages 94 and 95.

Power sources. Extending an inside power source to the outside is the same as extending wiring inside. You can tap into most switch, outlet, fixture, or junction boxes as long as the box contains a neutral

---

from the circuit distribution center to the common terminal of one switch; then connect the hot wire from the fixture or outlet to the common terminal of the other switch. Finally, run hot wires from the two remaining terminals on one switch to the two remaining terminals on the other.

Mount the switches and cover plates as directed on the facing page.

Installing dimmer switches

When shopping for a dimmer, be sure to buy the correct type for your fixture or fixture group: for example, a low-voltage halogen track requires a different setup than 120-volt downlights. Also make sure the dimmer can handle the required amount of watts.

If you're considering a dimmer for a fluorescent fixture, first make sure the fixture is equipped with rapid-start tubes; modern dimmers won't function with old-style preheat tubes. Then you must replace the ballast (transformer) in the fix-

ture with a special two-wire dimming ballast.

Most dimmer switches can be wired into existing circuits in the same way as the switches they replace. If the dimmer comes with short wires instead of terminals, use wirenuts to splice their free ends to the wires in the switch box. A typical three-way dimmer is shown below.

Three-way timer or dimmer with its own wires attached

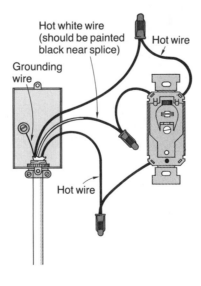

Hot white wire (should be painted black near splice)

Hot wire

Grounding wire

Hot wire

(white) wire and is not switch-controlled.

One simple method is to install an outdoor box back-to-back with an existing indoor box, as shown below. Pull the indoor device from its box, remove a knockout, drill a hole through the house siding, and screw the new box in place. Then feed NM cable through the hole, leaving 8 inches of cable on each side. CAUTION: Be sure to shut off power to the circuit before beginning work.

It's also easy to add a watertight extender ring to an existing outdoor outlet box—or even a porch light—and run new wire from there.

Installing an indoor switch and timer.
By wiring in an indoor switch and timer, as shown at right, you can turn outdoor lights on and off by hand or automatically from inside the house.

Types of outdoor cable and conduit.
Most local electrical codes allow the use of rigid conduit for outdoor wiring. Plastic conduit, though lighter and less expensive than steel, must be buried at least 18 inches underground. Steel conduit can be buried as little as 6 inches underground. Run two #14 TW (thermoplastic-insulated) wires through steel conduit, which is self-grounding; run three #14 TW wires (including a grounding wire) through plastic.

You'll need a fish tape (see page 84) to pull the wires, so plan to keep your layout simple. Special

Wiring an indoor switch and timer for 120-volt outdoor fixtures

Switch bypasses timer

Hot wire

Hot white wire (should be painted black near switch and splice)

Timer

Neutral wires

Hot wire

Grounding wires

Hot wires

From existing power source

To 120-volt outdoor fixtures

"pull boxes" along the way can make routing much easier. For details about working with conduit, see the *Sunset* book *Basic Home Wiring Illustrated*.

Some local codes allow the use of three-wire UF (underground feeder) flexible cable instead of rigid conduit. UF cable must be buried at least 18 inches underground. Work with UF cable in the

same way you work with non-metallic sheathed cable. Before covering the cable with dirt, lay a redwood board on top of the cable so that you won't accidentally spade through it at a later time.

Hooking up the fixtures.
Unless your new fixture includes a cover plate for wire connections, you'll need to furnish an accessible watertight box nearby. The drawing below shows a typical arrangement. In most locales, metal conduit is required between the fixture and the ground.

Fixture installation varies according to type and style. Be sure to follow the manufacturer's instructions carefully.

Adding a 12-volt system

To install a 12-volt system, you'll need a transformer, some two-wire outdoor cable, and a set of 12-volt fixtures. To activate the system, you connect the transformer, and perhaps a separate switching device, to an existing power source.

Wire thickness.
Most low-voltage outdoor fixtures use stranded wire cable. The size of the wires in the cable depends on the aggregate wattage of the fixtures to be served. Here are the appropriate sizes for some typical wattages:

#14 wire—up to 144 watts at 12 volts

#12 wire—up to 192 watts at 12 volts

#10 wire—up to 288 watts at 12 volts

120-volt outdoor wiring

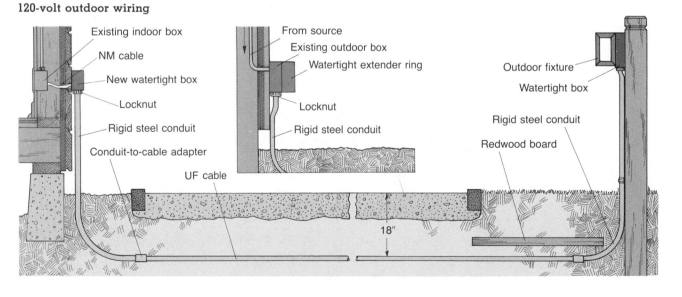

Existing indoor box

NM cable

New watertight box

Locknut

Rigid steel conduit

Conduit-to-cable adapter

From source

Existing outdoor box

Watertight extender ring

Locknut

Rigid steel conduit

UF cable

18"

Outdoor fixture

Watertight box

Rigid steel conduit

Redwood board

Installing a transformer. Most transformers for outdoor lights are encased in watertight boxes; but to be safe, plan to install yours in a sheltered location at least a foot off the ground.

If you don't already have an outlet into which to plug the transformer, use an outlet equipped with a ground fault circuit interrupter (GFCI). This device works like a standard outlet but cuts off power within ¼₀ of a second if current begins leaking anywhere along the circuit. The drawing at right shows how to wire an outdoor GFCI.

Though many transformers have built-in switches, some do not. Installing a separate switch indoors will probably prove more convenient than installing it outside. The drawing at far right shows how to wire a new indoor switch and existing power source to a new GFCI.

Most transformers for home use are rated from 100 to 300 watts. The rating shows the total allowable wattage of the fixtures serviced. The higher the rating, the more lengths of 100-foot cable—up to a total of four—the transformer can supply power through; each length extends like a spoke from the transformer.

To connect one or more low-voltage cables to the transformer, simply wrap the two bare wire ends of each length of cable clockwise around the screw terminals on the transformer—if the transformer accommodates more than

Ground fault circuit interrupter (GFCI)

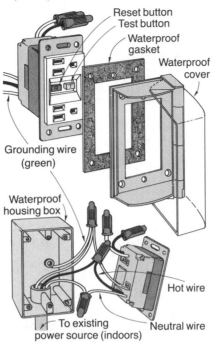

Wiring an indoor switch and power source to new GFCI

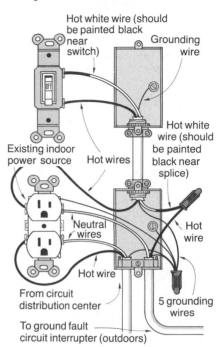

one cable, the screw terminals will come in pairs—and tighten the terminals. It makes no difference which wire connects to which terminal in each pairing.

Connecting fixtures to the cable. Once your transformer is in place and you've decided where to put the fixtures, you'll need to hook them into the cable or cables leading from the transformer.

With some fixtures, you simply pierce the cable with a screw-

down connector already attached to the back of the fixture. With others, you must screw an unattached connector to the main cable and to the end of a short cable leading from the fixture. Neither of these types of connector requires removing insulation from the cable.

A few brands of fixtures require splicing into the main cable with wirenuts (for help, see page 84). Use plastic housing boxes to insulate splices that can't be pushed back into the fixtures.

12-volt outdoor wiring

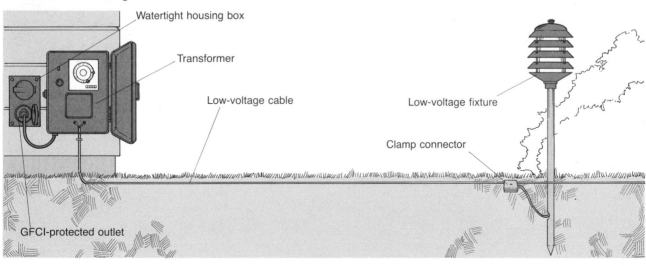

INDEX

Boldface numbers refer to color photographs.

A-bulbs, 10–11, **75**
Accent lighting, 5, 6, **23, 26, 27, 34, 41, 43, 50, 64.** *See also* Outdoor lighting
Aisle lights, **54**
Alcoves, 9, **73**
Ambient (general) lighting, **4,** 5–6, 9, **25, 28, 30, 37, 39, 41, 43, 46, 47, 50, 52, 53, 54, 64**
Architectural features, lighting, 8–9
Artwork, 9, **22, 27, 28, 29, 30, 33, 38, 50, 54, 56, 57, 60, 66**

Backlighting, **32**
Baffles, 15, **21, 29, 30, 40, 64**
Basements, **51–53**
Bathrooms, **64–71**
Bedrooms, **58–63**
Bookshelves, **31, 49**
Boxes. *See* Housing boxes
Bulbs, 10–11, **24.** *See also* by individual type

Cable, 84, 85–86, 94–95
Cable ripper, 84
Ceiling fixtures, 13, 14. *See also* Surface-mounted fixtures
Ceiling grid, **50**
Ceiling panel, **50**
Ceilings, lighting, 8
Chandeliers, 14. *See also* Surface-mounted fixtures
Circuit distribution center, 82
Circuitry, 82–83
Circuits
extending, 85–87
mapping, 83
Closets, **59, 63**
Codes, 81
Cold cathode, 12
Color effects, 6, 7, **23, 26, 29, 42, 62, 70**
Conduit, outdoor, 94
Control panels, 6
Cornices, 15, **44**
Coves, 15, **48**

Decks and patios, 17
Decorative bulbs, 10–11, **24**
Design, lighting, 5–7
Desks, **48–51**
Dimmers, 6, **28, 32, 33, 35, 37, 38, 52, 58, 59, 61, 76,** 93
Dining areas, **32–39**
Downlights, 16, **69, 74, 75.** *See also* Recessed downlights
Driveways, 16

Elbow fixtures, 15. *See also* Recessed downlights
Entryways
indoor, **20–21**
outdoor, **71, 72–75**
Eyeball fixtures, 15, **36, 61, 64, 66.** *See also* Recessed downlights

Fireplaces, **18, 24, 25, 28, 29**
Fish tape, 84
Fixtures. *See* by individual type
Floodlights, 16, **18, 20**
Fluorescent light
color rendition, 7
dimmers for, 93
fixtures, **18, 20, 21, 29, 31, 32, 39, 41, 42, 43, 44, 45, 46, 49, 50, 53, 55, 56, 63, 70, 71**
tubes, 10–12
Foliage, 17. *See also* Outdoor lighting
Framing projectors, 14, **76**
Furniture placement, 9
Fuses, 81

General lighting. *See* Ambient lighting
Glare, controlling, 6, 16
Globe
bulbs, 10–11, **52, 71**
fixtures, **26, 62, 69**
Ground fault circuit interrupter (GFCI), 95
Grounding, 82–83

Hallways, **56–57**
Halogen. *See* Quartz halogen
Heat lamp, **64**
High-intensity discharge (HID) bulbs, 10–11, 12
Housing boxes, 84, 85, 87, 93

Incandescent light
bulbs, 10–11
color rendition, 7
fixtures, **22, 35, 37, 41, 48, 49, 60, 61, 64, 67, 71, 73, 74**
"Incandescent" fluorescent tubes, **42**
Indirect lighting, 15, **31, 42, 48, 52, 56, 62.** *See also* Cornices; Coves; Soffits; Valances; Wall brackets

Kitchens, **40–47**
Knob-and-tube wiring, 84–85

Lamps, 12–13, **18, 23, 24, 25, 26, 28, 51, 60, 61**
Lanterns, **20, 35, 45, 57, 78**
Laundry area, **53**
Light levels, 6–9
Lineman's pliers, 84
Living areas, 8, **18, 22–31**
Low-voltage lighting
bulbs, 10–11, 12
indoor, 15, **18, 20, 22, 26, 33, 34, 35, 36, 38, 40, 54, 55, 62, 64, 65, 66, 67**
outdoor, 16, **72, 76, 77, 78, 79,** 94–95
Lumens, 7, 11
Luminous countertop, **70**

Main disconnect, 81
Marine lights, **54**
Masonry surfaces, 8
Mini-lights, 10–11, 14, **18, 36, 54, 55, 62, 66, 67, 78.** *See also* Low-voltage lighting; Surface-mounted fixtures
Mini-reflector spotlights, 13, **23**
Mini-tracks, 14, **37**

Mirrors, 8, **34, 63, 65, 66, 67, 68, 69, 71**
Mono-points, **20, 54**
Movable fixtures, 12–13. *See also* Lamps
MR-16 bulbs, 10–11, 12, **20, 23, 32, 34, 40, 48, 54, 58, 64, 65, 75**

Neon light, 12, **27, 46**
Neon voltage tester, 84
Niches, 9, **18, 27, 29, 54**
Nonmetallic sheathed cable (NM), 84

Offices, home, **48–51**
Outdoor lighting, 16–17, **18, 72–79,** 93–95
Outlets, **37, 46,** 91

Parabolic aluminized reflector (PAR) bulbs, 10–11, **38, 74, 75, 77**
Pedestal, lighted, **27**
Pendant fixtures, **4,** 14, **20, 35, 39, 50, 51, 53, 57.** *See also* Surface-mounted fixtures
Permits, 81
Pinhole apertures, 15, **34, 48, 57.** *See also* Recessed downlights
Plants, 9, **26, 37, 57.** *See also* Outdoor lighting
Plug-in outlets. *See* Outlets
Power source, 85, 87, 93–94
Professionals, 5, 81
Project ideas
built-in fixtures, **29, 31, 39, 44, 68, 70**
lamps, **25**
pedestal, lighted, **27**
pendant fixtures, **20, 57**
recessed downlights, **52**
shelf lighting, **47**
skylight lighting, **45**
stairway lighting, **55**

Quartz halogen
bulbs, 10–11, 12
color rendition, 7
fixtures, **23, 33, 35, 43, 54**

Recessed downlights
description, 14–15
indoor, **4, 22, 24, 28, 30, 33, 34, 35, 36, 37, 38, 39, 41, 43, 44, 45, 48, 49, 52, 53, 54, 58, 59, 61, 63, 64, 65, 66, 71**
installing, 89–90
outdoor, **72, 73**
Reflectance, 6
Reflector bulbs, 10–11, **37**
Reflectors, **21, 29, 57**
Room dimensions, 8

Safety, 16–17, 81
Sconces, wall, 13, 14, **37, 48, 58.** *See also* Surface-mounted fixtures
Security lighting. *See* Outdoor lighting
Service entrance panel, 81, 82
Sewing area, **53**
Shelf lighting, **47**
Sidelighting, **67**
Silvered bowl bulbs, **4,** 10–11
Skylights, 9, **45**

Slot apertures, 15, **58, 64, 65.** *See also* Recessed downlights
Soffits, 15, **22, 41, 68**
Solar rooms, 9, **36**
Solder gun, 84
Spas, 17, **77, 79**
Splicing, 84–85
Spotlights, 10–11, 13, **20, 22, 23, 28, 32, 57, 62, 74**
Spread lights, 16, **72, 77**
Stair fixture, outdoor, **73**
Stairways
indoor, **54–55**
outdoor, **72, 73, 74**
Strip lights, 14, **22, 35, 42, 48, 69.** *See also* Surface-mounted fixtures
Surface-mounted fixtures, 13–14, 88–89. *See also* by type
Surface wiring, 86
Swimming pools, 17, **76–77**
Switches, 92–93, 94, 95

Task lighting, 5, 6, **23, 28, 41, 43, 46, 48, 49, 50, 51, 53**
Texture, 6
Timers, 93, 94
Tools, 84
Track lighting
description, 14
fixtures, **20, 26, 28, 30, 33, 40, 50, 56, 57, 60, 63**
installing, 90
Transformers, **54, 55,** 95
Tubes, 10–11
Tubular bulbs, 10–11, **29**

Uplighting
indoor, 13, **23, 26, 37, 58**
outdoor, 16, **75, 76, 77, 79**

Valances, 15, **42**

Walkways, 16–17, **72, 74, 75, 78**
Wall brackets, 15, **31, 50, 71**
Wall fixtures. *See also* Surface-mounted fixtures
indoor, 13, **24, 26, 57, 65**
outdoor, 16, **74, 77, 79**
Wall-washer fixtures. *See also* Recessed downlights
indoor, 15, **24, 49**
outdoor, **73**
Watts, 11, 83
Well lights, 16, **72, 78**
Wet bar, **30**
Windows, 8–9
Window seats, 9, **59**
Wine cellar, **52**
Wire, working with, 84–85
Wire color-coding, 81
Wirenuts, 84
Wire strippers, 84
Wiring, 80–95
Work areas, **48–53**
Workshop, **53**